Praise for
LOSING MY FACULTIES

"A compelling look at the experience of teaching in high school . . .
a blow-by-blow account of the unmitigated bullshit an ambitious,
highly resourceful teacher must endure to continue doing his job . . .
Faculties should be on every teacher's personal reading list . . . full
of little triumphs and tragedies only teachers and students normally
witness."   —*Seattle Weekly*

"Engaging, irreverent . . . like catching up with an old friend who's
still amazed at having found a true calling, a job where 'every single
day I have at least some fun.'"   —*Yankee Magazine*

"[An] absorbing, almost journal-like memoir . . . Halpin writes passionately about his work. . . . This chronicle provides an irreverent
yet earnest look at the vocation its author clearly loves."
                                                        —*Publishers Weekly*

"Halpin shares his recollections with the kind of humor and affection reserved for a family scrapbook . . . a joyous trek through the
memories of one dedicated teacher."   —*Booklist*

"Halpin recounts the early days of his career and describes the ups
and downs of his many teaching jobs with verve and warm, witty
humor. . . . Portraits of secondary schools are rarely written in such
an informal, informative, yet jocular fashion."   —*Library Journal*

BRENDAN HALPIN, a thirty-five-year-old high school English teacher, is the author of the acclaimed memoir *It Takes a Worried Man* and *Donorboy*, his first novel. He lives in Boston with his daughter, Rowen.

Jon,

from Mom + Dad W.

Losing My Faculties

Losing

My

Faculties

A Teacher's Story

Brendan

Halpin

Random House Trade Paperbacks
New York

2004 Random House Trade Paperback Edition
Copyright © 2003 by Brendan Halpin
Reader's guide copyright © 2004 by Random House, Inc.

All rights reserved under International and Pan-American
Copyright Conventions. Published in the United States
by Random House Trade Paperbacks, an imprint of
The Random House Publishing Group, a division of
Random House, Inc., New York, and simultaneously in
Canada by Random House of Canada Limited, Toronto.

RANDOM HOUSE TRADE PAPERBACKS and colophon
are trademarks of Random House, Inc.

This work was originally published in hardcover by Villard Books,
an imprint of The Random House Publishing Group,
a division of Random House, Inc., in 2003.

Library of Congress Cataloging-in-Publication Data is available.

ISBN 0-8129-6951-0

Random House website address: www.atrandom.com
Printed in the United States of America
2 4 6 8 9 7 5 3 1

Book design by JoAnne Metsch

This book is dedicated to all my students,
especially the Halpin Advisory, Class of 2002:
Alicia, Bobby, Elizabeth, Jason, Jessica, Lisa,
Lurena, Melissa, Mike, Nakole, and Takako.

NOTE

Everything in this book is true. Well, anyway, I remember everything happening this way. Whether that's the same thing is an interesting topic but kind of outside the scope of this note.

So while every event appears in this book as I remember it, I did change the names of all the schools I worked in. I also changed the names of most of the teachers and administrators who appear in this book, and of every student who appears in this book. And, in a couple of cases, I combined people or pretty significantly changed identifying features in order to disguise identities.

PROLOGUE

Why I Do This

I'M HAVING A rough week.

No, I mean a *really* rough week. The kind of week when an improbable number of awful things have all happened at the same time—in the world, in my home, and in my school. The kind of week when you feel okay for about five or ten seconds when you wake up because you can't remember all the horrible shit that's happening to you, and then you remember, and you can't believe it's only Wednesday for God's sake, and you just want to crawl back into bed for a year or two.

Maybe you've had weeks like that. I hope not.

But today I am about halfway through a week like that, and after the weight of life falls on me, I stagger out of bed and eventually shuffle off to work. I'm a teacher.

I arrive at school, sit down at my desk, and wonder how the hell I'm going to do this today.

And then . . .

One of my ninth-grade classes is starting its summer-reading project. I explain the project, they take to it, they ask great questions, they do fantastic work, the period flies by. My seniors are finishing up *Medea,* and they're working on scenes they're going to perform tomorrow, and they're asking good questions and I'm talking to them about ideas, and the period flies by. My other ninth-grade section has just started their poetry unit, and they do a great job talking about what poetry is; they really listen when I tell them that poetry demands a different kind of reading from prose, and that period flies by too.

After school I go home and my wife, Kirsten, asks me how my day was. I think about how I spent most of it feeling horrible, and I'm about to tell her how completely miserable my day was, and then I remember how much fun I had working with kids today.

"Well," I say, "actually all of my classes went well today."

"That's good, honey."

"Yeah. So, actually, for two hundred forty minutes today, I wasn't miserable. For two hundred forty minutes of the day, I actually felt kinda good."

"That's not bad."

"No," I say, "I guess it's not."

So this is as good an explanation as any of why I do this work. On one of the worst days of my life, it was fun.

It brings me joy even when I'm surrounded by despair. I guess maybe that's love.

Part One

Prehistory

1

IN JUNE 1990, with the aid of some creative credit card use, I go to Taiwan on a bogus "exchange program" through my university. (My future wife, Kirsten, and I are the first and last participants.) The "exchange" is with some English-language institute in Taipei, and the idea is that my university sends them recent grads to teach for a few months, and they send students to the university's ESL program for a few months. Of course, the real idea is that the Chung Shan English Language Institute can put "Affiliated with Ivy League University" on its brochures.

I fell into this because I worked in the International Programs Office, and, being a senior with no ambition or clue what to do and six months before my student loans were coming due, I decided that spending six months in Taiwan would be a pretty cool adventure.

The only downside (apart from the fact that Taiwan in the summer is a bowl of heat, humidity, and pollution that puts even my native Cincinnati to shame) is that I have to work at the institute teaching English.

Well, maybe "teaching" is sort of a misnomer. Most of what I do is work in the children's English classes, which they attend on Wednesdays and Saturdays, when they only have a half day of regular school. There is a Chinese teacher here to run the class and really teach them stuff, and an American teacher to run language games. It's like a very specialized, makeup-free version of clowning. I'm good at it, but it gets old pretty quickly.

I also work the occasional evening teaching teenagers and adults. Here I am the only teacher in the room, and though the syllabus has every class planned out and it's mostly going through lame exercises in the book, it is a version of teaching. Sometimes I veer from the syllabus and actually talk to the students. I find that I enjoy the teenagers the most. I don't know why this is—I think I am just one of those rare and probably defective people who really enjoy the company of teenagers.

It is July, and I have an early-evening class of all teenagers. Years later I will still remember some of them—Julie, Jim, Kellie, and Angle, who pronounces it "Angel" (of course, they have Chinese names, but I never know them, which is kind of weird—it's like your French or Spanish teacher only knowing you as Pierre or Vicente or whatever name you adopted in high school language classes). I've been teaching this group for about a month, and they are finally comfortable enough to start speaking, and the lame exercise in the book evolves into something that very nearly approximates a conversation. Most of the students are speaking, their English is flowing pretty well, and they're asking questions about the grammar point and then using my answers—everything is just working really well. I am shocked when class ends because it feels like it just started.

I meet up with Kirsten, who was teaching across the hall, and prepare myself to leave the air-conditioning and step into the lead apron of swampy heat that is Taipei in the summertime. When the heat hits me, it's like a punch in the stomach. I've been here a month and I'm still not used to it. I immediately start sweating from every pore in my body, but I feel something else too. Something strange. Something I have never felt at the end of a day of work before.

I am happy and full of energy. I feel great—I'm buzzing tremendously and talking a mile a minute as I practically run down the street searching for some kind of cold beverage to save me from imminent dehydration.

"I can't believe this!" I say to Kirsten, who is looking at me "with stranger eyes," as one of our Chinese buddies would say. "I feel great! You're not supposed to feel great after work! You feel like shit, you go to happy hour to try and get happy, you don't get happy just from work!"

I worked the five previous summers in an insurance company and had a variety of jobs in college, and never, even when I watched TV for money in my dorm as a work/study "job," did I feel this good at the end of a day of work.

In my senior year of college I didn't feel very enthusiastic about pursuing any line of work because I just assumed that work was pain-in-the-ass drudgery that you endured until you had a few pathetic hours of free time in which to do what you really wanted to do. It just never occurred to me that work could be something you actually enjoyed. And then I get this glimpse of a world that few people are fortunate enough to know: the world in which work doesn't suck.

Work, it seems, can actually be fun.

2

I T IS 1992. I live in a tiny, mouse-infested apartment in Somerville, Massachusetts, a small city that borders Boston and Cambridge, and I am about two months into ed school in nearby Medford. I just got through with a year and a half of working at a computer company as a bottom-of-the-ladder, assistant-to-an-assistant mail sorter/photocopier/trash taker-outer. It wasn't horrible (except for one particular day when I was taking out the lunch trash and these bags of unused fish stock exploded all over me), but it wasn't exactly what you'd call fulfilling, and I sure as hell never felt great at the end of the day, so remembering my experience in Taiwan, I decided to go to ed school. So far it's not as horrible as everyone says. I have met some great people. Ten years later I will still be friends with two out of the thirty of them, which is really not a bad ratio. And we do nothing but think about teaching, which, I will find, is something you rarely have time to do when you are actually teaching.

I go to interview at the Boston public high school where I might get placed as a student teacher. The teacher, Gordon Stevens, wants to talk to me before he agrees to take me on, to make sure we can work together. He asks me why I'm interested in urban education. I give him a version of the truth—that this seems like where the real action is in education, the front lines, that if I have any talent for this at all, this is where I should be.

I do not tell him that I don't have a car and that this was the only placement I could get to by public transportation after my classmates snapped up all the Cambridge and Somerville placements.

The whole truth is that I really can't articulate why I feel like I want to teach here instead of in the suburbs. Certainly part of it is feeling like I want to make a difference, like it matters whether I go to work or not, which is something I never felt at the computer company. I remember having a number of really incompetent teachers (along with a handful of superstars) in high school, and I wasn't really harmed by them—basically anybody coming out of my small private high school started with enough advantages to be okay one way or the other. I feel like maybe that's not the case here, like maybe what I do could make a difference, like I would increase my own importance by working with kids who might have their lives changed by me. Yeah, so that's the liberal do-gooder really-out-to-make-himself-feel-important part, which is widely derided (unfairly, I think—isn't that kind of a win-win?).

I don't know. I'd like to say that I'm over that feeling completely now, nine years into my teaching career, but I know that one of the reasons I still love my work is that it feels important.

What I don't tell Mr. Stevens, because I haven't figured it out yet, is that I feel called to urban teaching (maybe a pretentious word choice, but it does feel that way—like somebody's tugging me to get into this, like I can't imagine working in a rich suburb or a private school, even though I never set out to be the Urban Education Warrior) not just because it will make me look big, and not just because I want to try something hard, and not just because it's where the action is. I want to do this because it's mine. Because I have spent my whole life in cities, because I can't seem to get away from the problem of how to live with people who aren't like you (or even people who don't like you), because I was brought up by a single parent in the city, because this is where I live.

Maybe Mr. Stevens understands all this, because he tells me he gets a good feeling from me and is looking forward to us working together. I'm looking forward to it too.

Of course, I'm also terrified.

3

OR THE FIRST half of the year, I'll be observing Mr. Stevens. I will take over two of his classes in the second semester. He is great at his job. It's not that he holds the class spellbound all the time—that's an overrated skill usually possessed by Cult of Personality teachers who are so in love with themselves that they convince the students to follow suit—he just oozes competence. And I am daunted by what it takes to achieve it. Even after what appears to be a very successful class, he retires to his "office"—by being in charge of purchasing office supplies, he has scored himself a supply closet in the attic and squeezed his desk between the boxes of chalk and paper clips, making him the only non-administrator in the entire building who has space in which to work when he's not teaching— and tortures himself, agonizing over what could have gone better,

what he could have done differently, what he will do differently tomorrow. It looks like a lot of work. I don't know if I really have it in
me to do this to myself every day.

Mostly I observe him with a class full of ninth-graders. One of
whom is a class clown named Trenton. He is obviously very bright,
but he's not doing his work and he mostly makes jokes about his
classmates. I write a paper about him and show it to Mr. Stevens.
He furrows his brow. He hadn't noticed half the misbehavior that I,
sitting silently in the back of the room, have recorded. Now he has
more stuff to agonize over.

One day I have a big cup of coffee right before class. I will never
do this again. Mr. Stevens gets the kids started on some sort of activity and then needs to leave the room—he has to talk to somebody
about something, perhaps relating to office supplies. "Mr. Halpin
can help you while I'm out of the room," he tells the class. This
is my first big moment, my first moment as a "teacher," and I am
paralyzed—I wasn't prepared to actually interact with the kids
when I left the house this morning! I'm just the Watcher! I watch,
and record, and imagine fearfully how I might deal with Trenton or
his classmates in every situation of every class. I can certainly handle the activity, but I hardly know these kids' names! What will I do
if they misbehave? What do they think of me? Who do they think I
am? I know when I was in high school, I probably would have been
instinctively contemptuous of somebody lurking in the back of the
room, and I probably would have tried to torture that person, just
out of that killer instinct that packs of adolescents possess. (At my
private high school we didn't have student teachers—they just
threw the twenty-three-year-olds with no experience right into the
classroom as full-fledged teachers. We did savage some of them.)
What if their relatively calm behavior arises only out of their respect
for Mr. Stevens? Will this room turn into a scene out of the first half
of *Lean on Me*, before Morgan Freeman starts carrying a bat and
Showing Those Tough Kids Who's Boss?

Trenton is having trouble with the exercise, and he calls me over for help. I get right up next to his desk and begin to explain—"Well, you see how the adjective goes here," or some such thing, and Trenton interrupts me. "I'm sorry, man, I don't mean to disrespect you, but you got that nasty Student Teacher Breath."

The class breaks up. I have no idea what to say. I am not yet secure enough to laugh at a joke like this. I probably try to pretend like I'm laughing, when of course I am horrified, so it probably comes out all fake, heh-heh. Whatever it is, I do nothing to save the situation except for not getting angry. Have I passed some kind of test, or failed it? Or both? I never get a chance to find out. Mr. Stevens returns, order is restored, and the class ends soon afterward.

Nine years later I see Trenton at the ice cream parlor in my neighborhood. He looks at me without a trace of recognition, but I know him immediately.

4

A T THE BEGINNING of the second semester the classes change, so the class of Mr. Stevens' that I will be in charge of is a group of twenty-seven tenth-graders. It is a writing class. I will be able to read and comment meaningfully on all of their papers because I have only two classes. I have no idea how I might manage to do that if I were teaching five classes of this size, which is what all the real teachers here are doing. For the first few days Mr. Stevens is in charge, and we are meeting in a science room with long tables and tall stools, only there aren't twenty-seven stools, so some kids are sitting on the heater over by the window, while others are on the floor. Somehow Mr. Stevens engineers a switch, and we end up in a French classroom that can just barely fit everyone.

On my first day of actually teaching this class without Mr. Stevens present, I get my big Test of the Student Teacher, which I fail miserably. I turn around to write something on the board, and somebody, somewhere (well, I know exactly which table it comes from, but since my back was turned, I do know enough to know I can't point the finger without enduring a twenty-minute debate about how I didn't see and I can't possibly be so unfair as to accuse someone without evidence), throws a piece of chalk. It explodes on the pipe that runs across the ceiling, making a really spectacular noise and showering dust all over the floor.

They have fired the test shot, and I must now define myself. I turn to the class and open my mouth, and this is what comes out: "You know . . . that is so not cool."

The class giggles, and right there I have lost them. Some good and even spectacular things will continue to happen in this class, but we will lose the equivalent of probably two weeks of time to disruptions because of how I don't handle this first one. I'm short; I look like I'm maybe sixteen; and, as it turns out, I have no idea how to talk like somebody you are supposed to respect. So the first thing that comes out of my mouth is all Sean Penn in *Fast Times at Ridgemont High*—Duuuuude! You're wreckin' my buzz!

Well, after this, the table of kids who threw the chalk decide that it's open season as long as I'm in the classroom. We are on the second floor with windows that open, so when it snows, they reach onto the ledges, make snowballs, and throw them next to me while I write on the blackboard. Spitballs, of course, make an appearance; at one point a basketball is passed around the room like a beach ball at a baseball game. I am surprised they don't actually do the wave. To their credit, I need to stress that this stuff is never thrown *at* me. Why bother? Throwing it near me is enough to provoke what they're after here—the angry-teacher show. I never again give them "not cool," but I try everything else: stern silence, screaming at the top of my lungs, swearing ("This is bullshit!" comes out after the basketball incident), talking to them after class. Nothing works. I should add that I was told by the woman at the university in charge of placing student teachers that I shouldn't even try sending anyone out of the classroom here. That the last time they placed a student teacher here, she sent a student out of the room for threatening her, and the vice principal sent him back to class five minutes later with a smile on his face and informed somebody at the university: "She doesn't know what she's doing." Well, of course not. She's a student teacher, genius.

When I tell Mr. Stevens what the placement lady at the university told me, he says, "Yeah, I remember that. That kid was nuts. We were all terrified of him." Luckily, none of my kids are what I would call nuts—that is to say, I'm not afraid of them in any real way—they're just making mischief. They remind me and everyone in the school's main office of who's in charge in this class at the end of every period, when they buzz the office intercom on their way out of the room. An annoyed secretary's voice comes on and says, "Yes, 205, what do you need?" and every day I have to say, "I'm sorry, the students pushed the button."

So I am completely on my own in terms of dealing with any kind of disruption. The school has no organized form of detention—I could ask a kid to stay after school, but there are no consequences if he doesn't show up. The school's discipline policy seems to boil down to: don't commit any crimes on school property. To be honest, I am not really sure about that one either. The school has a security guard, a pudgy forty-five-year-old woman who both the kids and I think is really cool, but she isn't really much of a deterrent.

One Wednesday night in our student-teacher seminar, we are talking about discipline, and my friend James, who is teaching in some wealthy suburb, says, "Well, I really didn't want to do this, but they just gave me no choice—I had to start writing names on the board."

I manage not to laugh, but I can't stop myself from one-upping him. "My kids threw a basketball at me," I say, because it is sort of true and it sounds better than what actually happened.

"Oh my gosh, Brendan, I don't know how you do it," my classmates say, and some come up to me after class to tell me how much they admire me for sticking it out in a tough situation. I guess it's pathetic that I need the ego strokes, that I need for my classmates to see me as the Heroic Inner City Teacher, but it does help me to find the energy to walk in every day knowing something is going to fly through the air and not knowing what it is.

Despite the daily disruptions, this class is actually where some of my first great successes as a teacher happen. I also have a senior class that gives me no discipline problems at all. This is partly because of their advanced age and maturity, but it also has a great deal to do with the fact that class begins at seven-thirty, and while it's not unusual to have ten or twelve students there by the time class ends at eight-fifteen, it is rare to have more than five out of fifteen at seven-thirty. I have to say that if I could have gotten away with this kind of attendance as a senior in high school, I totally would have.

The sophomore class, though, is after lunch, which may have a great deal to do with the bad behavior I see. Kids go to lunch, they get wrapped up in the stuff that's really important to them, and then it's hard to come back and focus on class. I don't mean to put them down at all in saying this. Remember high school? Lunch was the highlight of the day. Betsy sat near me today! And she offered me a chip *and* laughed at one of my jokes! Does that mean she likes me? Come on, get real, she doesn't like *me*. Then why did she offer me a chip? Answer me that! A lunch like that could keep my head out of class for the whole rest of the day.

And so it is with many of my students. And yet, somehow, I don't really know how, in spite of the stuff flying through the air and the daily performance of the Angry Teacher Show (now in its tenth smash week!), the students feel comfortable enough to allow the class to get real. The class is predominately black, with three or four white kids and a handful of Hispanic kids, and these kids want to talk about race. When I hand out Toni Morrison's *The Bluest Eye,* Juan looks at me, disgusted, and says, "So is this the black book? When do I get a Hispanic book?" Latoya, who in her introductory letter to me identifies herself as "a Nubian Princess," makes no secret of her hatred of white people. I, of course, am a guilty white person and feel I must Honor Her Rage, whereas if one of the white kids said the same thing about black people, I would probably—well, I was going to say kick the kid out of class, but of course I can't do that, but I would at least want to. So I don't give any speeches about how we need to respect everybody who's in the room, but luckily the other kids step up to the plate. Whenever any subject at all comes up, Latoya steers the conversation to something negative about white people, until her classmates start rolling their eyes as soon as she begins to speak and tell her to get over it until she tones it down.

Let me say that I am fully aware that my reliance on a bunch of fifteen-year-olds to keep the conversation appropriate is a really abject failure on my part.

One day Latoya is going off about how terrible white people are because they move out of neighborhoods when black people move in, and one of her classmates, who is also black, says, "Latoya, do you want white people living in *your* neighborhood?"

"*Hell* no!" she answers, and everybody, including her, laughs.

The kids write every day at the beginning of class and then share what they've written, and Terry always comes up with a "your mama" joke—Your mama's so fat, she wears size "continent" kind of thing, except usually funnier than that. He breaks up the class with these jokes, and his success inspires a host of lesser imitators, including John, who is one of the class's three aforementioned white kids. John has no success at all—his jokes are incredibly lame and inspire only groans and sometimes angry disgust in his classmates. One day John busts out with "Your mama's so black, she went to a night class and got marked absent!" I am getting ready to yell at him, and I'm really afraid I am going to have to pull Latoya off of him in about two seconds. How could a white kid be so dumb as to make such a totally racist joke?

The class explodes with laughter. Latoya says, "Good one, John," and he gets high fives all around the table. I have no idea what just happened.

One day I come in with a brilliant assignment: let's learn to write a letter to our congressman! We can learn the business-letter format *and* sound off on an issue that's important to us!

The students look at me like I have three heads. They openly ridicule the assignment: "Who the hell is my congressman? Why would he listen to me? They don't pay attention to people like me!" Hmmm. They are, of course, right, and it is pretty tough to give the "beauty and power of democracy" speech when I know that a letter from one of these kids isn't going to mean shit to anybody unless it's stapled to a four-figure check. I am initially annoyed with them for not going along with me, but when I go home that night, I realize that I can spend the next several classes banging my head against the wall, or I can follow them and try to make an assignment that matches their interests.

Most of our classes feature, in addition to stuff being thrown, a discussion about race that usually ends with me shouting over the three other people who are shouting that we are out of control and we need to stop talking about this now.

So I decide that we'll scrap the letter project and write essays about race and racism. The students can't wait to get started, and they all do the assignment (this is something of a miracle). Many of them have conferences with me about how to make a second draft, and a few kids do really spectacular work. It is a success. It doesn't solve anything or even get us closer to agreeing, but it does allow them to have a school assignment that actually means something to them and that teaches them something too.

Several days after the essay comes in, another spontaneous argument breaks out, when Latoya, in a rhetorical flourish that probably presages a career in politics, manages to slip "All serial killers are white; black people just don't do that" into what I thought was an explanation of comma rules. Karen, a white girl who has never responded to one of Latoya's pronouncements before, starts screaming about black people and drive-by shootings, and Terry and Kamira both start trying to yell at both of them at once. Dreading another Jerry Springer–style "discussion," I manage to get everybody silent, and I tell them to take out a piece of paper and write down what they want to say. Everyone will get to read, and nobody will get to react—I, the teacher, will say "Thank you" after each person reads, and that will be it. Everyone rushes to get out paper and everyone writes. Some don't want to read, but everybody who does is listened to. The written comments are more thoughtful and less inflammatory than what usually gets shouted in here, and I don't have to enforce the ground rules I've set up. They are just respected.

So, despite all the problems, on at least two occasions class manages to be serious and real. Nine years later, my memory is that the class with everybody reading their paragraphs and being listened to was my last class with them, but I know that can't be true. Still, it makes a nice ending, so I will leave them there.

5

MR. STEVENS HAS a conference to go to for two days, so the school decides to use me as an unpaid sub. This is a pretty widespread practice with student teachers. The university warned us about it and said we had the right to refuse, but we are here trying to make connections, network, and eventually find ourselves a job, and refusing to do a "favor" is not the best way to achieve this. Besides, the university has scant moral high ground on which to stand here—all of us student teachers are paying the university thousands of dollars so that we can go and work for free in local schools. I mean, yeah, we do have a three-hour seminar once a week, and it is great, but it is not exactly ten thousand bucks' worth of great.

So I take over Mr. Stevens' full course load, which consists of two senior classes and two sophomore classes. Of course, I am already teaching two of these classes. I am struggling with the sophomores, as I have already chronicled, and struggling too with the seniors, though in a different way—I just can't get them to do anything. This is a pretty universal problem with seniors in their last semester. Still, some students who did nothing for Mr. Stevens do some work for me, while others who worked for him shut down for me. Why is this? I am certainly not a better teacher than him. I think it's because part of our job is just personal alchemy—a lot depends on the mix of personalities. So Denise actually writes a paper for me where she never did for Mr. Stevens (then rips it up in disgust when I give her a C+), but Kendrick starts skipping class three days a week. Both students are black. Mr. Stevens and I are both white.

I go through two days with a full schedule, and it is the hardest thing I have ever done. At the end of the first day I go home exhausted. I have nothing planned for my classes tomorrow and no idea how I am going to fill forty-five minutes. I have to plan, I'm panicking, but I can't plan, I'm too tired, my brain won't work, and I can't believe I have to do this again tomorrow. I turn to my future wife, Kirsten, and start to cry. "I can't do it," I say. "It's too hard."

The next day, of course, I do it. I think this is one of those teaching rites of passage—not the unpaid subbing, though maybe that too, but the feeling that you cannot possibly walk into that building ever again at the end of one day, and then walking into that building to do it again at seven-thirty the next morning. That is basically the story of my entire first year of teaching.

Classes go badly. This doesn't surprise me; I am overwhelmed. I am also not getting the constant feedback I'm used to. I usually go to Mr. Stevens' supply closet on my free periods to discuss how classes go, but now, of course, he is not here, and I don't have a key, so I go to the first-floor teachers' lounge. Well, actually, it's a photo-copy room. Actually, it's a little piece of hell. I am stunned by the contrast between the supply closet, where Mr. Stevens and I talk seriously and thoughtfully about teaching, and this place, where the most benign part of the conversation centers on the alleged drunken exploits of Boston's mayor. "Oh, yeah, Raybo was so ham-mered he went in the wrong house," the teachers say, and "things Raybo does while drunk" becomes a ten-minute topic of discussion. It is unclear to me how these teachers—all of whom fled to the white suburbs in the seventies and now commute to teach in a city they no longer understand (there are black and Asian teachers at this school too, but they are not here. Where are they?)—got on a nickname basis with Boston's mayor. But the conversation takes a dark turn, and I soon long for more tales of Raybo's exploits once a student walks by, and one teacher says, sort of affectionately, "There he goes, the king of the con men," and then they are off for ten or fifteen minutes about the specific students they hate. This in-evitably evolves into more general complaints about kids today, and how things used to be different, blah blah blah. Luckily the talk fi-nally turns to stock portfolios and how long they have until they re-tire, and one teacher turns to me conspiratorially and says, "Yeah, this job actually pays pretty well for part-time work, heh-heh."

What planet is she on? How is it that I am working my ass off, am completely exhausted from less than two days of working as a full-time teacher, never have enough time to do all my correcting and all my planning, and she can sit there and tell me this is part-time work? It will be a couple of years before I formulate an answer to that question, and it boils down to this: teaching is a really hard job to do well and a really easy job to do badly. This is the dirty little secret that I hate to air in front of all the teacher bashers, but in some respects they are right—there are certainly teachers getting fulltime pay for part-time work, six hours a day, with three and a half months of vacation. I guess it's a pretty sweet deal, but how do they sleep at night?

The next day Mr. Stevens comes back and things get better, and the next time he is absent the school actually calls a sub (I think this is because he calls in sick and nobody at the school has my phone number handy). I also discover a perfectly good, perfectly isolated, perfectly empty teachers' lounge on the third floor. The black and Asian teachers aren't here either. Mr. Stevens tells me the white teachers stopped hanging out in there when the school wouldn't let them smoke anymore.

One of the students from the other senior class comes up to me at the end of the day and says, "Why weren't you our teacher today? We would have much rather had you than that clown town."

"Clown town?"

"Yeah, you know, Mr. Welch. He's such a clown town."

Well, I may not be much of a teacher yet, but at least I know that this isn't part-time work, and, more important, I am not a clown town. Whatever that is.

6

ONE DAY I am observing Mr. Stevens' senior class, and it is spectacular. They are reading Ibsen's *Hedda Gabler,* and while this particular group of students has had, shall we say, rather limited interest in this work for the last week and a half, today they are inexplicably fascinated and, without any prodding or leading from Mr. Stevens, have a thoughtful, passionate discussion about the morality of Hedda's suicide and suicide in general. For some reason, the students are totally into it, and they take off with the activity, and at the end of the class we can tell that something wonderful has happened.

Mr. Stevens, and this is the downside of his perfectionism, is miserable. He is miserable because he doesn't understand why today's class went so much better than yesterday's and (he doesn't say this, but he's been teaching long enough to know it) tomorrow's. If he could only figure out what happened today, then he could reproduce it daily, and he'd be much better!

He frets and we get into the elevator with another teacher, a tall, fat, Orson Welles–like man, and he inquires as to why Mr. Stevens' brow is furrowed. Mr. Stevens explains, and Mr. Welles, who is a fantastic raconteur, launches into this tale, which I think is apocryphal and which I can't make as entertaining as he does.

"Once Laurence Olivier was performing in *Hamlet*. On this particular night, he was brilliant. Everyone in the audience could sense that they were seeing something really special. The other members of the cast too felt themselves in the presence of greatness, and they, in turn, stepped up their own performances, so that everyone in the entire cast was performing flawlessly, though none, of course, as brilliantly as Olivier. He simply *became* Hamlet.

"After the performance and the riotous curtain calls, the cast and crew heard terrible noises coming from Olivier's dressing room. Finally one brave soul dared to open the door, and he beheld Olivier standing in the wreckage of what had been his dressing room, a look of pure rage on his face.

" 'Mr. Olivier,' the lad said, 'you were brilliant! What on earth could be wrong?'

" 'I don't know what I did!' Olivier cried. 'I don't know what I did!' "

The story is spellbinding, but Mr. Stevens is not impressed. "Teaching is not a performance!" he says to me later. "It's a profession! The things we do have to be reproducible if we ever want to have the respect that other professions have!"

I understand his point, but I'm with the fat guy on this one. Whether or not that story is true of Olivier, it's damn sure true of me.

7

MY STUDENT TEACHING ends a couple of weeks before school lets out. It has been a mixed bag, but I feel like I'm doing the right thing, and I definitely want to keep working in urban schools.

Many school districts come to interview at my university. I only sign up for one interview. I give up my spot at the Concord-Carlisle interview because Concord is almost an hour from my house, and it is a wealthy suburb. Cambridge and Somerville, the closest urban districts to my university, do not come to interview. The Boston Public Schools are scheduled to come. I sign up, one of only about three students who do. I wonder guiltily if my embellishing my tales of what happened during my student teaching has scared some of them off.

The day comes, and I get my suit on and trot over to the education building. There is a note on the door of the room where the interviews were to take place, saying that the interviews are canceled.

I go home disappointed, and in an act showing uncharacteristic gumption, I call up the Boston Public Schools and get transferred around for several minutes. Finally I reach someone straddling the line between surly and indifferent. "Hi!" I say. "I was scheduled to talk to one of your recruiters today on campus, but they had to cancel. I'm wondering if I could reschedule an interview for sometime later in the week, or maybe early next week?"

"Hold on," the bored voice says. I hold for two minutes. Finally she returns. "No. Just send your application in."

So I do. I even, in more shocking displays of gumption (you can tell how much I want this job), follow the advice of people who tell me not to mail anything but to take it down there and watch them put the "received" stamp on it, make follow-up phone calls asking if they have all my stuff and if they are scheduling any interviews. They never call.

8

I END GRADUATE school flat broke. I have hit up the financial-aid office for a little supplement in the springtime, which allows me to eat and pay my rent, but now it looks like I am back to the good offices of Kirsten if I want food and shelter for the summer. So I apply for jobs at two Upward Bound programs. These are basically academic summer camps for urban high school students. I have one interview that goes very well and I feel confident that I'll get the job. I don't.

I have another interview that does not go as well—you know the kind, where the interviewer is not giving you the nods and chuckles you're trying to elicit with your answers, where you just don't seem to be connecting for some reason. At the end of the interview, the woman says to me, "I know I really shouldn't be asking you this, this is really a postemployment question, but how old *are* you?" I really do look like I'm about sixteen. "I'm twenty-three," I say, and she says thanks, you know, it's just that I look so very young.

I'm convinced that there is no way in hell I am getting this job.

But I guess the woman liked me, or else she was afraid I was going to sue her for asking illegal questions in the interview (like I have money enough to sue anybody); whatever the case, she hires me.

I don't know it at the time, but this turns out to be a dream job. I teach three sections of writing to the kinds of kids who choose to go to school in the summer. I have no discipline problems, and because we are affiliated with a major university, I hold class in a room full of computers that actually work. This will never happen in any other computer lab I take my students to.

Many of my students are immigrants, so when we do a poetry unit, I have them write poems in English and in their first language, and it is one of the best assignments I ever give. A Salvadoran girl, Elena, writes a really moving poem in which she describes her school in El Salvador in minute detail, then reflects on the fact that she'll never see it again. Vinh, a Vietnamese boy, writes a poem about being on a rickety boat in the middle of the sea and being afraid. They read them in their native languages and then in English, and the class responds with awestruck silence followed by really vigorous applause. It's wonderful.

We also take field trips—I accompany them one day to see *Poetic Justice.* I am very excited because it is John Singleton's follow-up to *Boyz N the Hood,* which was preachy and anti-Korean but still pretty moving, and because it has Maya Angelou's poetry in it. Well, as you may or may not know, the movie is a complete piece of crap. It is incoherent, the poems suck and are randomly thrown in as voice-overs and are not important to the plot at all, and despite the shootings that begin and end the movie (or perhaps because of them), it is dull. In 2001 students will mythologize this movie, mostly because it has Tupac in it, but in 1993 I go with fifty high school students and the best thing any of them can say is, "Well, I guess it was kind of okay."

Despite the cinematic misfire, the work is incredibly rewarding. Except not financially. Because we are affiliated with a major university, somebody somewhere in some office can't find the grant money or doesn't want to release the grant money or some goddamn thing, so four weeks into this six-week program I still have not seen a dime. This doesn't bother most of my colleagues, because they have all just ended a year of teaching and have some money, and they know they'll get paid eventually. I, on the other hand, have nothing except some rather huge student loans coming due. I have to write a pathetic letter to the director saying how I really need to be paid because I need to eat, and she uses this as ammunition against whatever bureaucrat is not releasing the money, and we finally get paid.

During this whole program I am frantically applying for jobs. I want to work in the city, but it seems like that's not going anywhere. Nobody from Boston will return my calls, and my applications in Cambridge and Somerville also seem to be going nowhere fast. So I go through the same routine I went through last time I was unemployed—at first I concentrate on the jobs I want, and later I apply for any teaching job within fifty miles of Boston. I send out countless résumés, and I hear nothing. It gets to be mid-August, and I'm starting to panic. It gets to be late August, and I get incredibly depressed. I think I could be good at this. I have two top-notch schools on my résumé. Why the hell won't anybody call me?

A week before Labor Day, I go on an interview. The job is not my first choice. It's in a small city that is an hour from Boston on the commuter rail—not the kind of trip I'm eager to make, but it beats the hell out of commuting to the liquor store, which is all I'll be doing if I don't get a job.

The interview goes okay. I meet with the principal and the head of the English department, and I talk fairly coherently about why I want to teach and about some ups and downs I've had. They say they'll call me and let me know.

That night I'm sitting in my apartment watching *Beverly Hills 90210*. I mocked this show mercilessly as recently as last September, but Kirsten started watching it when I was at class on Wednesday nights, and now I'm hooked too. We are in reruns, but I didn't see the first go-round, so I am mesmerized as Donna—Donna, yet!—gets hammered at the prom and then is not going to be allowed to graduate until Brave Brandon leads a student revolt! Everybody walks out of class just as finals are about to begin, and they are chanting—

Brrring! "Hi, Brendan, this is Tim from Newcastle High. We were really impressed with you today, and we'd like to offer you the job."

"Donna Martin Graduates! Donna Martin Graduates! Donna Martin Graduates!"

"I'll take it!"

"Donna Martin Graduates! Donna Martin Graduates! Donna Martin Graduates!"

"Wonderful. School starts in one week."

Part Two

Newcastle

9

BEFORE I CAN get officially hired, I have to have an interview with the superintendent of schools. The train trip out to Newcastle is a very pleasant, one-hour ride. At one point the train goes right past this scene of really stunning natural beauty that actually seems to be enhanced by the gigantic, beautiful, peaceful homes right next to it. I walk about fifteen minutes from the train station up to the main office of the Newcastle Public Schools and have an interview with Frank, the superintendent, which he announces at the beginning is completely a formality. "You've got the job, by the way," Frank says to put me at ease, and while I appreciate it, I wonder, well, why the hell did I just drag my ass all the way out here, then? He asks me some questions I don't remember, and I give standard kiss-ass answers.

I fill out some papers and go home clutching the piece of paper that has my salary written on it: twenty-two thousand dollars. This is shit money even in 1993, especially considering the five and a half years of student loans I have to pay back. The train ride home is a very long one, and the rich people's mansions that seemed so pleasant and peaceful on the ride up seem like giant evil monuments of injustice, and it's all I can do not to flip them off as I try to calculate how much I'm going to owe for student loans, how much I'm going to be bringing home, and how much I think I'll need for rent and food. I do the calculations. It looks like I may have enough money to buy some clothes, but a car is out of the question.

What the hell have I done? I've just taken a job fifty miles from my house, and they're not going to pay me enough to get a car? I could probably afford a commuter rail pass, but the commuter rail doesn't run out of Boston in order to get people to the far suburbs by seven-thirty in the morning. The first train stops in Newcastle an hour after school starts.

Shit. I'm fucked.

What really depresses me is that I was so broke during grad school, and I was really looking forward to working so that I could sort of have enough money, and now it looks like I'm going to be broke all the time again.

I get home, and Kirsten has that excited smile on her face like you do when someone you love just got a new job, and she says, "What's wrong?" as soon as I walk in the door, and I say, "I'm going to make twenty-two fucking thousand dollars and it's in East Jesus and they're not going to pay me enough to get a car and I'm going to be broke all the fucking time and what the hell am I going to do?"

I also have my schedule. It turns out that Newcastle High sorts its kids into three tracks, and three out of my five classes will be the lowest level. These are the kids who once would have dropped out of school to work in Newcastle's once-thriving, now-dying industrial base. Now there are no jobs for unskilled sixteen-year-olds, so they have to stay and get a diploma. I am undaunted because, though I am an hour away from the city, I am the Great Urban Education Warrior! I will make them love English and me! I will show this school that kids they have labeled as stupid can excel!

I still don't know how I'm going to get up there every day when new-teacher orientation starts. I rent a Festiva, Ford's bottom-of-the-line shitbox at the time, and drive up for it. The system has hired a bunch of new teachers this year, and they put us all on a school bus and give us a tour of town, they feed us shitty lunches, they take our picture for the local paper, and we have meetings. Five years later I will forget everything but the bus tour. I meet the other new teachers, but I don't really connect with them. They are mostly female, which would normally be a point in their favor as far as I'm concerned, but they are . . . well, they are the kind of people who can have a conversation about which funny-named drinks they like. A long conversation.

A few days after orientation we have a whole-faculty orientation. Every teacher from the Newcastle school system files into the auditorium at the middle school to hear speeches. The big highlight is the speech from Frank, the new superintendent. Frank is an old, thin, bald man who tries to affect a folksy manner that can't quite cover his obvious desire to cut the heart out of anyone who crosses him. His speech makes it clear that he has no earthly idea what year it is.

He opens with a joke about the newspaper. "I'm new in town. I almost fired my secretary because every morning she comes into the office waving the paper and says, 'F.U.L.' It took me three days to figure out she was talking about the *Federated Union Leader*!" Polite chuckles.

"I'm just kidding, Ethel, as long as I'm here you'll always have a job. As I'm sure many of you know, Ethel is fantastic." Burst of applause.

"And then there's the assistant superintendent, Vito—those of you at Dockside Elementary remember your old principal . . ." Applause. "I call Vito the Godfather."

'Cause he's Italian! Get it?

(Later I will find out that about half of the student body is Italian too. Does Frank know this? Does he care?) The speech goes on in this vein for another fifteen minutes or so as we hear of all the hard work that the Godfather has been doing, but seriously, the Godfather's great, I couldn't do this job without him, I have to say that or I'll end up at the bottom of the river, ha ha.

Then Frank gets to his big inspirational moment for the teachers. This is what he says: "No dungarees! Dress professionally, and that means no dungarees!"

Well, I don't know about anybody else, but I'm sure as hell fired up to teach after that stirring call to arms. Also, who the hell says "dungarees" anymore? My eighty-one-year-old grandmother says "blue jeans." *Dungarees.* Honestly.

Luckily, this will be the last I will see of Frank and his archaic ethnic and sartorial vocabulary until the end of the school year. Also luckily, I meet a woman who works at the middle school who also commutes from the Boston area, and she is looking for someone to carpool with. Great! I wasn't planning to wear my dungarees to work anyway, and now I have a way to get there! Looks like I'm set.

10

BRIDGET AND HER husband live in Cambridge, where he works. I now live in Boston. In order to get to Newcastle High School by seven-thirty, I have to leave my house at quarter to six. I ride the subway, and it is a very different experience from when I worked at the computer company. When you ride the subway at seven-thirty or eight, you are riding mostly with office workers in suits. Before six it is all construction workers and custodians. Even though I am so tired I want to curl up on the nasty floor of the subway car, I also kind of like it. We're the men who work hard for a living every day—not like those office-working wusses sauntering into work at eight o'clock! No sir! This is the hour when *men* who work *hard* ride the train! Men like me!

I change trains, then emerge in Cambridge's Central Square, where I hop into Bridget's car and hold on tight as she drives like a bat out of hell and gets us to Newcastle in forty-five minutes.

We have a personable enough relationship, though there are a few strains. One is that she listens exclusively to classic-rock radio. This is fine for the first week or two, but after that, hearing the same seventeen songs over and over again starts to drive me insane, so that I want to tear my hair out when I hear the opening chords of

"Maggie May" for the tenth time this week. (We seem to get that one both going in and coming home.)

Also, it's just difficult for me to not have control, not just of the radio but also, and most important, of when I get home. Some days—actually most days—I am dog tired and can't bring myself to do any work after school, and I have to wait for hours because Bridget has track practice or is involved in some marathon meeting, which they seem to have daily at the middle-school level.

A couple of times I get calls from her at quarter of six in the morning saying she can't make it to work that day. I should just call in sick myself, but although I was a total slacker in my corporate jobs, I am John Freaking Calvin when it comes to teaching, so on those days I call up my friend Mary, the Newcastle High band director, who lives a twenty-minute bus ride from the end of the subway line, and she gamely agrees to take me with her.

This gets frustrating, but what can I say? It's Bridget's car, it's her schedule, and it's not like I have any other options—I'm not bringing anything to the table here except forty dollars a month in gas money.

Still, we talk a lot about school and other things—she is much more conservative than I am despite living in Cambridge, so I try to steer away from topics like "It should be harder to get divorced," and "I don't really have a problem with gay people as long as they don't flaunt it."

By the end of the year we are pretty sick of each other, mostly just because I cramp her style, she makes me wait forever, and we are not the kind of people who would ever become friends or have even one forty-five-minute conversation, let alone 180 of them, under different circumstances.

A year later I will see her in the mall, and by this point my annoyance has disappeared. I'm not going to invite her over for dinner, but I really have no bad feelings toward her whatsoever.

Apparently the feeling isn't mutual. "Hey, I know you!" I say in that tone of pleasant surprise as I see her walking toward me. I stop for the exchange of pleasantries, but she just looks at me out of the corner of her eye, gives a deadpan "Oh. Hey," and keeps walking.

11

I T IS PRETTY clear from the word go that Newcastle High is not a healthy place. There is, of course, the fact that it is technically under the stewardship of Mr. No Dungarees, who is about as popular with the staff as you might expect; on the first day of school I see a teacher dressed in jeans. "He can't tell me not to wear jeans," I overhear him saying. "That's not in the goddamn contract."

The atmosphere here is poison. I can tell at my first department meeting. I sit quietly as Tim, the department chair, speaks, and Nancy, Stephanie, and Margaret all send him these hate waves. Dan says something and Tom, sending similar waves, visibly shifts in his seat. Only Olivia and Hope sit there looking just bored and not hateful.

What the hell is going on here? I have no idea, and I don't know who to ask. Stephanie takes me aside to welcome me to Newcastle High and throws some completely gratuitous shots at Tim into the conversation. Obviously I can't come to Tim's defense, because Stephanie, whatever her political status, seems formidable, and I don't want to make an enemy. The fact that Tim hired me makes me clearly suspect anyway. I try something noncommittal like, "Oh, well, heh, I don't really know anybody yet, I guess I'll find out . . ." and run out of the room.

One thing that I learned from the menial office jobs I did before teaching was to always be kind to the people on the bottom of the ladder. This strikes me as basic human decency, yet it seems to be beyond most people's abilities. But I remember being the piss boy and feeling like I deserved the same amount of kindness and re-spect that everybody else got, so I always try to return the favor. I have to admit that I'm not exactly Saint Francis here—another thing I learned from my experience in corporate America is that the people on the bottom of the ladder, especially the secretaries, run things. So being nice to them is not only the right thing to do, it can also be very helpful when you need a favor or a rule or deadline bent. And it's not a tough thing to do either—it mostly just involves talking to people like they're human beings.

Anyway, I end up having a nice relationship with Janice, one of the custodians. Janice is a graduate of Newcastle High, about thirty years old, and loves to talk. I mean *loves* to talk. Every day after school I find her talking to Mary, the new band director and occa-sional ride giver, and the closest thing I have to a peer here, and I frequently join in because I am too fried to do any work after a long day of teaching, and even on the best of days, Newcastle Middle School gets out an hour after the high school, so I have to wait for Bridget anyway.

Janice is very kind and helps Mary out immeasurably—she es-sentially becomes the number-one band-booster volunteer as a sec-ond job. (Well, at least I think it's a second job. I very rarely see her actually cleaning anything.) And she also helps me out because she knows everybody and everything.

"Why does my whole department hate each other?" I ask her one day after school.

"How much time do you have?" she answers. I tell her I'd like an under-thirty-minute version, if she can deliver. She can. What she tells me is that Tim has just become department head this year. Be-fore that, Stephanie was the department head for years and years. During the summer there was some kind of bloodless coup—Tim was appointed department head as a sort of compromise candidate between the Stephanie lovers and Stephanie haters, since he appar-ently was neither. Unfortunately, nobody told Stephanie until she showed up to check on a book order over the summer and found the locks changed on her office and all her stuff in the hall. Classy.

She also tells me why Tom hates Dan. Dan currently lives with a woman many years his junior. She was one of Dan's students and moved in with him only a few weeks after her graduation from Newcastle High. This was five years ago, so she's twenty-three now and Dan is forty-three. Dan is not reputed to have had affairs with any other students, but Tom still can't forgive him.

Wow.

Well, I guess that's what I get for asking.

12

IT'S MY SECOND day as an employee of Newcastle High School. I'm still driving my rental car, and it's still only teachers in here—the kids will arrive tomorrow. I am in the book room, rooting through the stacks looking for stuff to teach. Tim promises to try to dig up the curriculum, but he will never deliver this, and anyway, it becomes obvious pretty quickly that the curriculum is fictional. Everybody pretty much does whatever the hell they want.

This is both good and bad. My pals from ed school sometimes tell tales of having to turn in next week's lesson plans to their principal every Friday, of ironclad curriculums filled with crap they hate doing, and I was terrified that I would be subject to the same scrutiny. It looks like I'll be able to run my classes any way I want, which is great, except it means I have to build curriculum for three grade levels from scratch. What do we expect the kids to know at the end of the year? Nobody can tell me. The only thing I know for sure is that they have to read a Shakespeare play every year, even in sophomore year, which is their American-literature year.

I have been given some big fat anthologies, but these always suck, and my problem is compounded by having level-three classes. The level-one and -two students have some relatively new-looking anthologies, but the level-three kids get the castoffs—the old editions that are all beaten up from years of use. Well, the school has a limited budget, so why spend lots of money on books for kids who won't read them? Right?

Anyway, I am there in the book room, which turns out to be a kind of treasure trove—all the books from back in the seventies when English teachers got to teach cool stuff they liked in "English electives" are still here and basically intact—the electives trend came late to Newcastle and left early. Olivia, another English teacher, is there picking out a selection of Dumbed Down Classics for her level-three kids. These are books with recognizable titles that have been modified to contain about a fifth-grade vocabulary and reading level: *Poe for Dummies,* and such things. These, I will discover, are all her classes "read." They also sit silently and do a lot of worksheets and take a few tests. Olivia is a prime proponent of the "you don't bug me, I won't bug you" school of teaching.

But I don't know this yet. All I know is that she turns to me in the book room and says, "Oh, this particular Dumbed Down Classic works really well with the eleventh-graders."

"Oh, well," I say, "I was actually looking at this book of short stories. I think I'll try that first."

Olivia looks at me like I'm dumb as dogshit. "These are level-*three* kids," she says.

"Yeah. Well, I think I'm going to try this."

"Suit yourself," she says, looking at me the way you'd look at someone who announced he was going to ride a tricycle down the expressway. When she leaves, I just plop down on the little rolling stool and put my head in my hands. I remember all of the great people I was in ed school with—people who cared, people who believed in kids, people I liked talking to. I was happy, excited, and proud to start being a teacher and looked forward to working with the same kind of people I went to school with. Instead I get this lady. Shit. What am I doing here? I have that feeling I haven't had since my first day of camp the summer after fifth grade—oh, shit, I'm stuck here, I want to go home, I want my mommy.

My opinion of Olivia, and by extension Newcastle High, is not helped by the end of each school day. After my last-period class with the juniors ends, I stand by the windows and look at the parking lot. It is the rare day when Olivia and Hope don't beat all the students out of the parking lot at two o'clock. I really don't know how they do it—they must actually stand by the door waiting for the bell to ring, or else they've been doing it for so many years that they just have an instinctive sense of when the bell will ring and they can start walking at the perfect pace to be crossing the threshold of the school at the exact second when it starts. Why the hell, I think, is this lump just taking up space here? She is obviously just going through the motions, she obviously doesn't care about kids, why doesn't she pack it in?

Then one day Janice tells me the story of the Suicide. Last year at Newcastle High, a fourteen-year-old ninth-grader blew his head off in the lunchroom. Many of my sophomores watched it happen. Janice tells me how Tom stood there ineffectually passing out tissues all afternoon, how for a whole week afterward all the kids just drifted in and out, mostly talking to crisis counselors and rarely going to class, how the kid's friends couldn't decide between grief and anger, how they walked around saying, "Why did he want me to see that?" and how, the minute it happened, the minute the shot went off, while the rest of the lunchroom was paralyzed or screaming, Olivia, whose husband had died only a few months earlier, had run to the table and cradled the dying boy in her arms, saying softly, "It's okay, honey, it's okay, it's going to be okay," and stroking his bloody hair until he died.

13

S O MAYBE OLIVIA doesn't fit too neatly into the box I made for her in my mind. Neither does Bob, a science teacher, recently divorced, who eats lunch every day surrounded by a gaggle of teenaged girls to whom he talks about his love life. He's not hitting on them or anything, so it's not like it's illegal or even immoral—it's just creepy and kind of sad. I hear him in the hall one day calling out to a fifteen-year-old female student: "Will you marry me when I grow up?" Then one day he brings his son to school. His son has autism, and this guy is just so affectionate and patient, and the very idea of having any kid at all, much less an autistic one, fills me with terror at age twenty-four, and I am really impressed with Bob. But I still think it's creepy that he talks to teenaged girls about his love life.

Whatever my opinions about my colleagues, I am able to put all those concerns on the back burner once classes actually begin. Having three level-three classes is pretty standard practice for new teachers—everybody foists all the classes they don't want onto the new kid. One of my level-three classes is a group of sophomores I see first period. This class ends up going pretty well, overall. They are a good-natured group of kids, and class starts at seven-thirty when they're still half asleep. Actually, one girl is frequently more than half asleep. She has a newborn son and comes to school two or maybe three days a week, says something like, "My son is sick . . . he was up all night . . ." and promptly falls asleep on the desk. I don't have the heart to wake her up. I'm kind of in awe of her—a seventeen-year-old single parent. After a while she just stops coming at all.

My second level-three class is fifth period, right before lunch. It's a group of ninth-graders, fourteen boys and two girls. The first day, one of the students looks around at all the kids in the class and says, "So. I guess this is the retard class, huh?"

One of the kids in this class, Rick, is actually a sixteen-year-old sophomore. He failed ninth-grade English, so he takes that with me and tenth-grade English with somebody else. He seems to have some legal difficulties—he comes in from time to time after having been absent with a note saying he has had a court date. One day he comes in, practically hugs me, and says, "I got my chins dropped!" I am too new to teaching to know he's talking about a "Child in Need of Services" order.

Rick is also really, really smart. He is in level-three English, though, because of his behavior and legal troubles. One day he does something unacceptable—I think punching a classmate or something—and I kick him out of class. He literally throws a desk—mindful of the basketball story, I don't want to say he throws it *at* me, because he just does it out of frustration and I don't think he means it as an attack on me, but I do have to do a quick sidestep to avoid being hit.

Rick's placement, I will find, is pretty typical of level-three classes; there are always kids in them because they have behavior problems, and putting them in a class where the pace is too slow for them doesn't usually help their behavior problems, and their behavior doesn't help the kids who are in these classes because they have a tough time learning.

Thirteen of my sixteen students have IEP's, or "individualized education plans," which means special education. Students on IEP's are required to be mainstreamed—that is to say, they must be integrated into the regular education program and not segregated in "pullout" special-education classes. So my students have all been "mainstreamed" into the same English class, effectively making me a special-ed teacher.

I have no special-ed training.

So the deck is stacked against me, but I also do my share of fucking up. I have the students write for a few minutes at the beginning of the class, and I tell them it is their time to write whatever they want. What I mean is that I'm not setting a topic, so they can write what's on their mind. So a kid decides to test it on day three or something, and says something like, "I feel like shit." I object, and he says, "But you said we could say anything we want."

And here is where thinking too much kind of screws me up. I think, well, this exercise is about having them overcome their fear of writing, about empowering them to feel that writing is a form of communication that is real for them, and how can I do that if I stifle their authentic voices? How can I gain their respect if I go back on my word? I am tortured by this for the whole year, and in the meantime, they are swearing when they read their freewrites, and I am doing nothing about it. I'm sure this doesn't make it any easier for me when I try to get some order in the class, and I am so befuddled by this "dilemma" that the solution—write anything you want, but you can only say things that are appropriate for class—doesn't present itself, and indeed the very idea that I have the authority to insist on appropriate language and even to define what appropriate language is doesn't occur to me, because I am all about student empowerment, man, because these kids have been beaten down by the educational establishment (true enough) and they need me to do things a new way and help them to own their education. I make the terrible mistake of reading Jonathan Kozol's *The Night Is Dark and I Am Far from Home,* which is all about how the people who perpetrated the My Lai massacre were mostly trained in public schools, and how we shouldn't be training kids to be unthinking war criminals (I'm paraphrasing), which is okay, and which I guess I agree with, I mean, I'm as anti-war-crime as the next guy, but when you are trying to teach something to fifteen kids who think they're stupid, you really do need to be somewhat in charge or all hell breaks loose.

But philosophically, I want to empower them, I want them to be free citizens rather than obedient automatons, and so I am just terribly uncomfortable with the reality of my authority. So basically my authority has no reality in this class.

I demonstrate this vividly to the class in the first week, when I make the mistake of mentioning to the vice principal, who's new on the job, that I'm kind of struggling, that a couple of the kids keep trying to provoke Rick to make him go off for their amusement. "I'll give you some theater," he says, and the next day he comes up and literally screams in these kids' faces—his voice echoes down the entire school, I mean people who teach on other floors ask me what happened later on because they heard the commotion, and one of the kids, who was just being goofy, almost starts to cry, and the other kid just looks really, really hard.

Tom comes up to me the next day and says, "Jesus, what the hell was Bruce doing? That was embarrassing." Yep, and ineffective too. Strangely enough, yelling in a kid's face and publicly humiliating him doesn't always turn him into a model citizen. And it's all very fine for Bruce to come in and scream at kids, but I'm the one who has to spend forty-five minutes with them every day, and now they know I called this shit storm down on them, and so I look weak and don't even have the advantage of appearing to be on their side. So nothing changes.

I try all kinds of different seating arrangements, assignments, and structures, and nothing really works. Until the end of the year, this will be the class I will dread, the class that makes me cry at the end of the day, the class that makes me feel like the biggest failure. It is not at all unusual for me to lose half of my class time to disruptions. People swear, people punch each other, people don't listen. I have to send two kids out for sexually harassing the one remaining girl in the class—they can't stop talking about her "beaver." I write "sexually harassing classmate" on the little slip they take to Bruce, and later Bruce confronts me and says how if I use the words "sexual harassment," there is this whole legal procedure that he is obligated to go through, and I say, Okay, well, this is a pretty clear-cut case of sexual harassment, so go to town with your procedure, and whatever the big, scary legal process is, it never seems to result in any consequences accruing to the offenders apart from the standard two detentions they get for getting kicked out of class. By this point in October, they have already gotten enough detentions from all their classes to take them through Christmas.

By the springtime, they will be untouchable—they are already assigned detention through the end of the school year. At this point, though, they will have started frequently coming to class high, and though I will be ashamed of this later, I don't really do or say anything about it. They are heavy-lidded and unusually cooperative, and unlike when they are not high, they are not stopping anybody else from learning. And it is the worst-kept secret at Newcastle High, where the school grounds extend to the woods, that kids get high out there. My two sexual harassers are a pretty small percentage of the total number of stoned kids.

Still, these kids are fourteen. And they are getting high in school. And I look the other way and do nothing to try to help them because it's much easier for me. So much for my heroic-teacher movie.

One day it's almost the end of fifth period, and we are sitting in a circle, and at *exactly the same moment* two things happen. First, Dennis, a short, ten-year-old-looking kid prone to making up stories about his ninja training, shouts out to his classmates, "Hey, is anybody else here in the KKK?" His classmates, all white and no beacons of racial tolerance themselves, react with immediate and sort of surprising anger.

"KKK?"

"Shut up!"

"What the hell?"

"Let's beat him up!"

"Yeah!"

And, on the opposite side of the circle, Henry, a kid who dresses in all black and wears his hair in a black-dyed Mohawk, pulls out a box cutter and slices down the length of his arm. His arm begins to bleed, and Henry makes a great show of licking the blood off. His classmates respond with predictable shock and disgust.

"What the hell is he doing?"

"Oh, that's sick!"

"Let's beat him up!"

"Yeah!"

At that moment the bell rings, and everybody runs out of the room for lunch. I go straight to the vice principal and tell him about the box cutter, and he goes into the lunchroom, where Henry is calmly eating with his friends as if nothing has happened. The vice principal demands the box cutter and hauls Henry up to the school psychologist's office.

This is before the days of "zero tolerance." If Henry tries this stunt again after 1995, he will be summarily expelled from school rather than taken for counseling.

So Henry now has mandatory counseling, and he is furious. He glares at me through every class; he is a black cloud sitting in the corner, sending off waves of hatred. This, I will discover, is a pretty typical pattern for the troubled teen: "Here is my cry for help!" quickly followed by "How dare you heed my cry for help! I hate you!"

One of Henry's friends comes up to me a couple of days later, giggling, and says, "I heard Henry cut his arm in class to make you think he was a psycho!" All I can think to say is, "Well, it worked," but I manage not to.

A week later Henry walks up to me at the end of class, gets right in my face, and says, "Mr. Halpin. You don't like it when I cut myself, do you?"

"No, Henry, I don't."

"Well, how do you like *this*," he says, sticking his left thumb in my face, grabbing the nail with his right hand, and ripping the nail right off.

I manage to respond with atypical aplomb.

"Well, Henry," I say calmly, "I don't like that either."

I write up the incident and give a copy to the vice principal and the school psychologist. A few days later, Henry stops coming to school.

That's the worst thing that happens in this class, and it's usually not that bad, but it's usually at least pretty bad. I barely know what I'm doing and the class is out of control for at least part of every day, but strangely enough, we do get some real learning done. Unlike Nancy across the hall who reads everything aloud to her level-three classes (so it's basically forty-five minutes of story time and the kids never actually read the books), I insist that they read, and some kids do. I insist that they write, and all the kids do. Nobody else in this place does this with level-three classes. I photocopy packets of their writing, which they proudly read aloud to the class, and as much as I've screwed up, I am proud of what I've done, at least compared with what I know my colleagues are doing with their classes. The kids getting story hour or worksheets might have been a whole lot quieter than mine, they might have sworn a whole lot less, and they probably threw fewer pieces of furniture (they were probably stoned in similar if not greater numbers, though), but they also didn't do any reading or writing. And this is the trade-off I will continue to make throughout my teaching career. Though I will get better at the discipline stuff, I am fundamentally a marshmallow, and I will trade a little bit of chaos for a little bit of student involvement. It's pretty easy to run an orderly class, but if you want kids to really write and to really get involved, it gets messy.

In the springtime I get to assign the kids to their next year's English classes, and I bump everybody I think has even a hope of surviving academically up to level two.

The following year, when I am no longer working in Newcastle,

Tom will call me and tell me that Rick has been running around the school going, "Where's Halpin? Bring back Halpin! What did you do with him?"

The year after that, one of my students will mention that she is dating one of my period-five students from Newcastle. "He says he really liked you, that you were a great teacher." It's nice to hear this, but it also makes me sad. I knew nothing. I couldn't keep order in the class. What does it say about his other teachers that this kid remembers me as a good one?

14

I AM GIVEN a somewhat less than completely warm welcome from most of my colleagues in the English department. I have to "float"—that is to say, I don't have my own classroom. Instead, I have my five classes in four different classrooms. This leads to a lot of lost papers.

This also leads to some friction with my coworkers. I have my first-period class in the room usually occupied by Nancy, who writes all her notes for the rest of the day all over all of the blackboard space in the room before first period. "Oh, here," she says, pointing to a space of about two square feet surrounded by the notes she will give her classes (the level-two and -one classes, of course—level three gets story time), "you can use this." I am cowed by her experience and her thinly veiled hostility. She was the youngest teacher here before I came, and continues to show off her ever-thickening legs with short skirts; she seems, though she is forty-one, to have staked out the "I'm the young, hip one" territory and does not appreciate my intrusion on her turf. Because she intimidates me, and because, deep down, I know I am a fraud—I have no idea what I'm doing! I leave work every day with a complete blank in my mind about what's going to happen tomorrow! I can't stand up for myself or they might find me out!—I never tell her that she doesn't own the room, that it's a workspace and right now I'm working in it, that I'll use however much of the goddamn blackboard I feel like, and she can like it or fucking lump it.

Margaret comes to me and in no uncertain terms tells me that when the desks are moved out of the neat rows she has them in, it is not enough to simply put them back in rows—they must be back in the exact spot they left, that the corner of the third desk cannot be two inches to the left of the corner of the first desk.

A couple of times Nancy is teaching next door to me and my class, for whatever reason, gets loud, and she does not have the courtesy to speak to me in the hallway—rather, she opens the connecting door and yells directly at my class. Stunned to be yelled at by "a real teacher," my kids fall silent.

So I am not exactly Mr. Popularity with my colleagues, and while Nancy is the only one who has actually come in and yelled at us, I know other people are disturbed by the noise in my classes. Sometimes this concern is justified—my classes are frequently out of control—but other times my students are loud because they're excited about what we're doing, and the idea that learning is anything but a quiet, orderly activity is completely foreign to these people, so they think I have a problem.

And being friendly, helpful colleagues eager to help a young person succeed in the profession, they of course take me under their wing and offer to help me out. Ha! Actually they rat me out to the boss.

One day after a department meeting Tim comes up to me and says, "Pete and I"—Pete is the principal—"are a little concerned about you. We understand you've been having some discipline problems."

"We understand"? What the hell does that mean? Well, it means my colleagues in abutting classrooms have been complaining about the noise. Back-stabbing old fuckers.

"So I talked to Pete"—great, pal, when were you going to talk to me?—"and we agreed that I would get a sub for my classes tomorrow and follow you around to yours."

I somehow manage to respond, though I am so angry and humiliated I can't believe I can actually speak.

I go home and cry and cry as Kirsten—still my future wife, but it's now less than a year in the future—tries to comfort me. "I fucking hate that place!" I sputter out between sobs. "I never want to go back there again!"

At five forty-five the next morning I leave the house and go to do it again. Now, I like Tim, Tim has always been nice to me, but I'm really nervous. Before school starts I go to seek out Tom to ask him what he thinks this means politically. I pick Tom because I have two classes in his room and he has always been supportive, he is never a bite in the ass about what's on the board or where the desks are, and the fact that he hates the student-fucker guy kind of makes me respect him.

"Well," he says, "Tim and Pete both really like you and want you to succeed. I don't think they're looking for documentation. I think they're really trying to help. They're just being incredibly clumsy about it." Tom turns out to be right, and this conversation marks the beginning of what will become a really nice friendship. Tom and his wife, who is also a teacher, will frequently take me out for coffee after school while I'm waiting for my ride, and he proves to be someone I can really talk to and someone who continually encourages me. His reassurances—"You're doing a great job, I can tell by what the students are saying," "We really need more people like you who are serious about this job"—will sustain me through a very tough year.

But right now I have to go through an entire day being observed. I don't know if the students have some sort of extrasensory perception that makes them want to protect me, but all my classes go really well. The students do the activities, nobody misbehaves seriously, even period five goes smoothly, and at the end of the day I feel good. "I had a great time," Tim says, "and it looks like you're doing a great job."

A few days later I get a follow-up visit from Pete, the principal. He comes only to my seventh-period class, level-three juniors. I really like this group, and they can be thoughtful and genuine and do really good work. They can also be gigantic pains in the ass. At the end of the third quarter I will have to cook the grades a little bit to make sure that the whole class doesn't fail—once springtime hits, they will just stop turning in papers. But today Pete is here, and we are in the middle of a poetry unit, and I have prepared a little response sheet for them to do. I thought of this sheet at the last minute, and I am really nervous because I don't have a clear plan of attack with the poem we are doing today.

The poem is Wordsworth's "We Are Seven," in which the speaker goes and meets a little girl who insists over and over that there are seven children in her family, though it quickly becomes clear that five are dead.

Pete loves to read aloud; unlike most principals, he covers detention himself, and spends the time reading aloud to the detainees— short stories, poems, or whatever he happens to be reading for pleasure at the time. He is good at it. I ask him to read "We Are Seven." He does a fantastic job, reading the poem in a quiet, serious way and really bringing out the pathos.

I give the kids their response questions and ask them to write. They tear into the paper like they are possessed. They cannot wait to get their thoughts down.

After a few minutes I ask them to speak, and what happens next is probably the best class I will ever have. At least, eight years later, I will be unable to think of any single class I've had that even comes close.

As they talk about their reactions to the poem, the students start bringing up family members they've lost—siblings, cousins, parents. They speak honestly and movingly, and, best of all from the perspective of an English teacher, they keep coming back to the poem—"It's like it says here in line ten" or "When the little girl says . . ." By the end of the class, they have done as thorough a job analyzing the poem as I could have hoped for, and better yet, they've done it while talking about how the poem relates to their lives. Today my class was both rigorous and real, and I love my students. It is the class period that makes my year, that makes me think, well, maybe I'm not so bad at this job after all. And *the principal* was here to see it!

Several weeks later, one of the vice principals will come into the same class for one of my official evaluation visits. He sits there for about ten minutes, which is the point at which I stop the class because it has become clear that not a single student in the room has read the five-page short story I assigned them for homework. I stop class and announce that since they have come prepared to do nothing, nothing is what we will do, and that means they cannot sleep, they cannot do homework, they cannot talk, they cannot do anything but sit there. I will try this trick a few more times in the coming years. It is really effective—it's torture.

At the end of the class, after the vice principal leaves, I say, "You know, I work really hard every day for you guys, and I get *shit* back from you."

This is not fair, because of course they have already given me what might be the best class of my career, but I am really angry and scared about the evaluation, and they are suitably shocked by my scatological language. It does improve their homework-completion rate slightly for a week or two.

I end up getting a glowing evaluation. The vice principal basically has no choice in the matter. He is required by the contract to make three visits to my class, and he will never make another one. If he says so much as one negative thing, I would get to grieve the evaluation as unfair, and I would win automatically because he hasn't made the visits. So I, a first-year teacher with a lot of potential, okay, but with a hell of a lot to learn, become perfect on this piece of paper.

Tim's shadowing me for a day, Pete's "We Are Seven" class, and the vice principal's ten-minute visit constitute the entirety of my supervision in my first year of teaching.

15

GET UP at five. I'm usually home by about four-thirty, though when Bridget becomes track coach, this is more like five. I fall on the couch for a few minutes, make dinner, do an hour's worth of reading papers or planning classes (I find that I can't neglect this hour or I will wake up at four-thirty worrying about the papers I haven't corrected or the class I haven't planned), watch an hour of TV (by this point I am planning my week around Wednesday's *90210*, and I will continue to do so through Kelly's illicit romance with Dylan, Kelly getting burned in a fire, Kelly joining a cult and trying to become *Homo lucens*, and will finally give up when either Kelly or her artist boyfriend or both are drug addicts), and fall into bed by nine-thirty.

I never go out on Friday nights. When I get home on Friday, I sleep for an hour, and then I'm in bed by ten. I'm just starting to get interested in *The X-Files*, which comes on at nine during these years, then I quickly lose interest because I always fall asleep halfway through. Kirsten gets us tickets for a Friday-night performance of Handel's *Messiah*. I fight to stay awake, battling to keep my chin off my chest even when the trumpet sounds and the dead shall be raised incorruptible.

I feel kind of like a monk. A *Beverly Hills 90210*–watching monk, but a monk nonetheless. There are days when I can't believe how much I suck at this job. Yet I never even consider throwing in the towel. I don't really know why.

I guess part of it is that usually, most of my day doesn't really suck that bad. While the ninth-grade class will be a puzzle I can't solve all year long, and the junior class, apart from the "We Are Seven" day, continues to give me fits with their refusal to do work, I do have three tenth-grade classes that actually go okay. These are the classes where I don't have to spend the bulk of my time on discipline, so I learn, however slowly and painfully, what works and what doesn't, what kind of questions will get interesting answers, and how to manage a group of kids every day.

My first-period class is fine, but it never really gets exciting—it is never terrible but also never really soars. Whereas my last-period juniors are just about jumping out of their skin. I wonder what seeing these groups of kids at different times would do, and I even join the volunteer committee that is looking at new scheduling options. It forms after we get a presentation on block scheduling and its many advantages, and I am intrigued, so I join the committee only to find it packed with people who joined with the express purpose of making sure the schedule stays exactly as it is now until the end of time. I go to only two meetings, but the vice principal is the chair of the committee, so my participation gets me a nice couple of sentences in my end-of-year evaluation.

My second period develops a very nice atmosphere. With a few exceptions, the kids in this class are the misfits, and I am always drawn to the misfits. They dress in black every day (they are friends with Henry but don't share his penchant for either confrontation or self-mutilation), they smoke in the woods at lunch, they wear

shockingly disgusting T-shirts for their favorite death-metal bands
(one that stands out in my mind featured a skinless male corpse
performing oral sex on a skinless female corpse—eccch), and they
are smart and interesting. One day I find a bunch of them under the
bleachers at a pep rally, and I say to them, "Look, I'd rather hang
out under here too, but we all have to go join the crowd out there."
We emerge to find the student body screaming its approval as one
of the football players stomps on a stuffed bulldog, which is the
mascot of hated rival Northton High.

My seventh-period class is my biggest—twenty-seven kids—but
also the best. The kids do their work, mostly, and we always have
lively discussions. In the beginning of the year, we are reading some
horrible Puritan shit because I am plowing through the American-
literature textbook, and they ask me why we have to read this, and
I launch into this long thing about how literature helps you to understand a country, blah blah blah, and I don't think they really buy
it, but they are impressed enough by my sincerity to stay with me
for the rest of the year. The kids in this class are so good that, well,
two of them skip school one day in order to get Pearl Jam tickets,
and when they come back the following day with no documentation, no phone call from home, nothing, everybody just assumes
they were sick and they get excused absences.

My fondest memory of this class is watching Roman Polanski's
Macbeth with them. We had read the play, and I got this version
without watching it first, so I didn't really know about how the
witches are naked and elderly. There are certainly communities in
which showing this movie would have been enough to terminate
my teaching career right there.

Fortunately, Newcastle isn't one of them, and so I don't get in
trouble for the geriatric breasts, though I do lose some sleep worrying whether I will. Anyway, at the end of the movie, Macbeth is de-
capitated on-screen and his head rolls across the courtyard, and
when this happens, the entire class bellows its satisfaction, and

when that happens, Pete the principal comes in and explains how they are having some kind of school-committee luncheon with the superintendent right over there in the library and how they can hear us bellowing and how he's really delighted that they're enjoying school, but he needs to ask them to be quiet. I think he means it. His face reminds me of nothing more than my own face when I had to chase the death-metal fans out from under the bleachers. He'd much rather be in here bellowing at Macbeth's death, and he'd love for us to scream about it, but he has to take care of this political bullshit.

Apparently he doesn't do a good enough job taking care of political bullshit, but I'll get to that shortly.

So, yes, my ninth-graders are out of control, and yes, all my classes are way too easy, and yes, there are some days where I don't feel like I've done anything worthwhile in any of my classes, but those days are rare. Most days, I feel like I get something done, and every single day I have at least some fun. Even when the juniors are driving me nuts, I get a kick out of them. Yes, I see teenagers at their worst, but I also see them at their best, and I get to laugh every day and I get a buzz off of work that I damn sure never had at the insurance company or the computer company.

I know that this is the job for me because I keep forgetting to get paid. This happens all the time. I simply forget to go to the office to pick up my check. I have no idea when payday is. This particular feeling will evaporate once I have a child and a mortgage, but right now I'm still sort of pleasantly surprised whenever I get a paycheck. Oh, you mean I get paid for this too? Now, part of this is the training I received paying thousands of dollars to teach as a student teacher, but it's also that I can't stop thinking of work as something you suffer through until you can do what you want, and of a paycheck as the thing that justifies your wasting so much of your miserable life under fluorescent tubes instead of doing what you want all day. But now I *am* doing what I want all day. *And* they pay me for it!

16

N APRIL 15 I get a pink slip. It regrets to inform me that I will not be hired back, blah blah blah. I don't panic because every teacher in the building with less than three years' experience gets one of these, and they all look the same, and everybody—principal, vice principal, department head—tells us not to worry about it, it's just a formality.

The contract requires teachers to be notified by April 15 whether they are being hired back next year, but the town never has its budget passed by that time, so because the school system has no idea what their money will look like, they fire all the first-, second-, and third-year teachers just to give them some wiggle room in their budget.

"Don't worry about it," they say, "everybody gets hired back."

What they don't know, or aren't telling, or don't believe will have any effect, is that the newly elected mayor of Newcastle has just eviscerated the school budget. Of course, he's done this in a really sneaky way—not by taking money out but by adding line items. So while, for example, snow removal (no small expense in Massachusetts, especially this year when we do not have a full week of school between February vacation and April vacation due to weekly snowstorms) has always been done by the town snowplows and has been considered a town expense, the mayor is now billing the schools for the use of the town snowplows, effectively cutting thousands of dollars from the school budget. He's shifted a number of items over from the town general fund this way, thus squeezing the school budget considerably. Sneaky bastard. I don't live in Newcastle, but I'll bet "screwing the schools" was not his campaign slogan.

Well, a few days before school ends, one of the vice principals tells me not to worry, he's pretty sure that I'll be getting hired back. But, he adds, he is sort of out of the loop right now because he's resigned his position as vice principal to return to teaching science. I don't know if this is a good decision or not, but I do know that it means somebody in the science department is getting screwed. The department has two new teachers this year, and one of them is getting fired because this guy decided he didn't like his promotion.

On the last day of school, the other vice principal goes around the final faculty meeting handing out the "Just kidding! Actually you are getting rehired!" letters, and smiling and joking with the recipients. I watch as he hands them all out, and I am waiting for him to come over, and by the time he gets to me, his hands are empty. "I'm sorry, Brendan," he says, and keeps walking.

What?

Wait a minute.

What?!

Later I will find out what went on behind the scenes. The word came down from Mr. No Dungarees that there were going to be some budget cuts, and could department heads please present some enrollment figures justifying all their positions. Well, apparently the vocational department, which enrolled all of about twenty kids, cooked its numbers pretty severely so as to have it appear that its moribund program was actually growing next year—nobody knows exactly where these kids were coming from, they would have had to raise the dead to achieve these numbers, but there you go. Apparently, as a new department head, Tim did not know how to play the game at this level or something, but anyway, the bottom line is that my position was new this year, I hadn't replaced anybody but had been added due to growing enrollment, and somehow all the masses of undead voke students were not going to take English, but anyway, I got canned.

There were some other budget cuts in the school that Pete, the principal, didn't agree with, and he and Frank went back and forth until Pete finally wrote a letter of resignation and said I can't continue to work for you if you don't listen to what I say about what's best for the school, and Frank, slavering, grabbed the letter out of Pete's hand and said, "Yoink! Thank you very much!"

At the end of the day I am frantically asking everybody for recommendations in between kicking myself: "Dumbass! Why'd you believe them? Dumbass! Why didn't you start applying for other jobs? Dumbass! Don't you know these motherfuckers are always lying to you?"

Pete says he'll be happy to write me one (and who better—he witnessed probably my greatest class ever), and then he asks me what I'm doing in the summer, and I tell him I'm planning on job hunting and hanging out at home, and he gets this kind of faraway look in his eyes and says, "Yeah, the city is great, especially in the summer. You get your girl, and a picnic, and a ninety-nine-cent bottle of Spanish red and head down to the river . . . you feel like a king."

But I feel pretty much like a chump today. Mary takes me out to lunch at this gargantuan Chinese restaurant that is several times larger than the whole of Newcastle High School, with louder décor and, ultimately, I decide, more class, and this makes me feel a little better. But only a little. It's June 24, and I have no job.

Part Three

Northton

17

A FTER GETTING LAID OFF, I go into a frenzy of sending out résumés and cover letters and recommendations, except that Tim, the department head at Newcastle, seems to be too feeble to both write and send me a recommendation. I call him periodically, and he blathers at me about how he can't get it typed, he's trying to get his wife to type it. This goes on for weeks. I end up calling Tom practically crying in frustration. Every school on earth asks for three letters of recommendation, and I have only two and it certainly looks funny that my department head won't write me one. Tom promises to call Tim and yell at him for me.

I never get the recommendation.

What I do get through the good offices of Tim is a job. So I guess I can't really complain about the recommendation too much. His wife, Terri, teaches at Northton High, so she got my résumé sort of bumped to the top of the pile, and I go in for an interview and knock them dead.

Once again I get the job one week before school begins. Once again the school has no real curriculum in place, so I will have the wonderful freedom to do whatever I want along with the horror of having no assistance in creating a curriculum from scratch. Well, what the hell, I've done it once already, I can probably do it again. This also pays better than Newcastle—enough that I can actually afford a tiny car in which to commute and not listen to classic-rock radio. Of course, I'm still not quite living my dream of being a Great Urban Educator. In fact, Northton High is actually a much less urban school than Newcastle High. Northton is not a wealthy town, but it is an all-white, all-Catholic suburb, and while it has none of Newcastle's mammoth summer homes for the wealthy, it also has none of Newcastle's unemployed heroin addicts. So it's a much more homogenous, typically suburban place than the weird mix that was Newcastle and is therefore farther from my urban education dream. On the other hand, Northton is twenty miles closer to my home, so at least I'm moving closer to the city geographically, if not demographically.

I am replacing some guy named Dan Rather, no relation, ha ha, who was legendary for doing almost no teaching at all. One guy in the department tells this story of how he walked through Dan's room at the beginning of class to get a book or something and heard him droning out the attendance, and when he went back into the room fifteen minutes later, he was still droning out the attendance.

I have one senior class, and though I am undoubtedly the kind of guy they would beat senseless for fun if I were their age, the boys in the class decide that I'm cool. One of them even writes a poem at the end of the year called "The Halpin Blues," which is this awesome paean to me that features the inspired couplet "He's got a badass goatee/Hell no, he ain't no wannabe!" How many jobs offer you a chance to get something like that?

Anyway, I am required to stand in the hallway before class and impose order with my fearsome five-foot-four, 140-pound frame. What actually ends up happening is I hear a lot of stuff teachers are never meant to hear because so many of the kids don't have males as short as me programmed into their teacher radar yet. Frequently Kevin, future author of "The Halpin Blues," and Kent stand in the hallway with me.

One day a girl who dresses in all black and has some kind of attention-grabbing dye job walks by and Kent looks over at Kevin and says something along the lines of "What the hell's wrong with that freak chick?"

It's the kind of horrible shit that this girl, who is actually a really nice, sensitive kid, gets all the time, and I let Kent have it. "Hey. Don't stand next to me if you're going to be cruel to people. I don't want any part of that—it's disgusting to me." He looks at me with a complete lack of understanding—I thought you were cool, why are you sticking up for the freak chick? After that he stops standing next to me in the hallway.

A few days later Northton High gets its first Hispanic student. He is dressed in what at the time is typical urban fashion—cartoonishly baggy pants and some kind of sports jersey. He has the misfortune of walking down the hall to his first class in front of Kent. Using his un-erring instinct to punish the different, Kent calls out, "Hey, Snoop Dogg! Hey! What up, Snoop Dogg? Hey!" and like that. The His-panic kid whips around and throws a punch. It's the only one he will land. Kent is all over him and beats him bloody, breaking a pane of glass next to the fire door with the kid's head. Later I have to step over the blood to get to class.

The Hispanic kid, it turns out, is not from Northton, he's on some kind of school-choice deal, and we, it turns out, don't want his kind around here, these criminals come in here and get in a fight the first day, no sir, he can go right back to where he came from and go to school with his own kind, thank you very much.

Kent is back in school in two days.

He wins the battle, but this war will not go well for his side—in five years about a third of the all-white student body will be dress-ing like the kid Kent beat up, coming to class with DMX CD's in their Walkmen and Fubu shirts on their back. Future Kents will call the boys "wiggers" and the girls "hoochies," but it won't have any teeth. There are just too many of them.

18

S O I REALLY like my seniors, mostly. I mean, one of them does write a poem in my honor, but, like last year's juniors at Newcastle, they just don't really have it in them to do any work. Well, no—two girls do everything I ask them to do and do it well, but the rest of the class just barely scrapes by, and it's very difficult to run a class when nobody is doing the work. *Frankenstein* is the most spectacular failure I have with them—it sounds interesting and everybody's excited to start it, and then we all find out how much it sucks. It doesn't work as a horror story, the plot mechanics are embarrassingly bad, and the heavy-handed philosophical allegory just doesn't interest any of us very much. After this they are kind of wary of anything I give them, and we limp through to the end of the year.

I also have three ninth-grade classes, which range from very good to okay depending on their size. The class of seventeen goes very well. The class of twenty-seven is okay, respectable, but there is frequently just too much chaos in there. I actually see the same phenomenon when the teachers sit in faculty meetings: when one person is talking to a large group, no individual in the group feels a responsibility to hold up the other end of the conversation. So it somehow doesn't feel rude to turn and talk to somebody while the person up front is talking. I do it myself all the time. Which is fine, but it just means that in a class of twenty-seven, if you have ten people doing that, there's too much chaos for anything to get done.

Once I do something that could certainly get me fired—a stupid stunt that I won't repeat. The class is talking and talking, they won't listen, I'm standing there like an idiot trying to get their attention, and nothing is working. Finally I pick up one of those gigantic English anthologies and fling it down on the linoleum. As predicted, it hits the floor with a very loud and satisfying crack that certainly gets the attention of the class. As not predicted, it hits the floor with a great deal of force at kind of an angle and goes sliding across the floor and hits Christine in the foot.

Sure, it's an accident, and no, it doesn't hurt her at all, but it's totally indefensible, and, should Christine choose to make an issue of it, it could certainly end my teaching career. There is really nothing

I could possibly say to justify this. So the intended spectacle of me creating a loud noise to get the attention of the class becomes a spectacle of me begging a fourteen-year-old girl for forgiveness. She seems kind of embarrassed by my contrition and insists that it's no big deal.

I don't get fired for this.

This same class has one of the two students in nine years that I just won't be able to reach any accommodation with. Now, it's become kind of a point of pride with me that I can find something to like in even the most difficult kids. I am somewhat puzzled by this, because while an adult just has to say one mean or offensive thing for me to write him off forever as an asshole, I can always see the good in a kid, even one who says cruel and offensive things on a daily basis.

Except for Jimmy. Basically the kid just lives to get on everybody's nerves. To be fair, he certainly doesn't focus on me—he will happily annoy the shit out of one of his classmates too. I have his sister Jamie in another class, and she says to me one day, "I just can't stand him. Everybody says, 'Oh, yeah, when you guys get older, you're gonna love each other,' but it's not true. I hate him!" I can see why. He just pushes buttons until the pushee loses it. And with most kids like this, you can, at some point, have a normal conversation, particularly if it's one-on-one with no audience. So I try a few one-on-ones with no audience with Jimmy, but even with nobody else there to impress, he smirks at me, he mocks me to my face, he says, "Oh, yeah, sure, Mr. Halpin, whatever you say, Mr. Halpin," in a smarmy, sarcastic way.

So I lose it with him on a semiregular basis. I always count it as a win for him if he gets me to kick him out of class or if I yell at him, and he usually wins. The only time he doesn't is once when I'm wearing a tie with some kind of floral pattern on it. "Oh, Mr. *Hal*pin," he says in this stereotypical lisping gay voice, "I just *love* the *flowers* on your *tie*. Don't you just *love flow*ers?"

I am annoyed, not because I give a shit if this kid thinks I'm gay, but because, you know, I'm trying to talk about *To Kill a Freaking Mockingbird* here, and we have only forty minutes, and I'd rather not spend it talking about whether my tie is butch enough for him. "Jimmy," I say, "are you trying to imply that I'm homosexual?"

The class falls dead silent in an instant, that loaded, anticipatory, something-we'll-discuss-at-every-reunion-is-about-to-happen kind of silence, and Jimmy looks stunned. "Um . . . well . . ." He is uncharacteristically speechless.

"Are you trying to say that I'm homosexual?" I repeat. Jimmy still can't bring himself to speak. If I were his peer, he'd doubtless say yes so we could fight about it, but he doesn't have a script for this, so he continues to sputter. I continue calmly, "Because I'm not. Now, when Scout and Jem find this stuff in the tree . . ." Everybody is stunned by my refusal to get mad about this. It doesn't make any cultural sense. This is a marked contrast to one of my colleagues, who still happily tells the story of how some kid said, "You're a faggot!" on his way out of class one day and he chased the kid into the playing fields, tackled him, and brought him back to the principal's office, which, if true, should totally put my mind at ease about clipping Christine's foot with a textbook.

My ninth-grade classes end with what begins as a spectacular failure in *Romeo and Juliet*. I drag them through it line by line as we read it in class, I explain that yes, you're supposed to giggle when he says, "My naked weapon is out," I explain every single sex joke in the play, of which there are many, and yet it is dead, it is boring, it sucks.

So at the end of the unit, I split them into groups and have them "translate" a scene and perform it. The results are spectacular. One group in particular does a great job of turning *Romeo and Juliet* into something like *Beavis and Juliet*. So, "Turn, villain, and draw!" becomes, "Shut up, butt-munch! Get your sword out!" I take them out into the courtyard to perform on the first day, and it goes really well, and the kids are tremendously excited about the chance to go into the forbidden courtyard (Northton High's very nice courtyard will be closed to students for as long as I work here). The next day I get the word that the math teachers were complaining about the noise in the courtyard, so the rest of the performances take place indoors. It's significantly less fun, but this assignment is still a big win for me, and it's a nice way to end the year. Years later kids will still talk to me about it, and I am amazed—I mean, yeah, I thought it was fun, but nothing extraordinary, yet for many of these kids, it's the single wackiest thing they have ever done in an English class. Which is kind of sad.

19

I ALSO HAVE a level-one sophomore class here in my first year. These are the kids who are expected by the school to excel and then attend prestigious private colleges, whereas the level-two kids are expected to go to less prestigious state colleges, and the level-three kids—well, if they can just graduate, the school will feel that it's done its job. Which is an indicator that the Northton community is a little more upscale than Newcastle.

Level-one classes are typically the province of the veteran teachers who have paid their dues teaching the low-level kids when they were younger, so it's kind of unusual for me to get a level-one class, and it's almost unheard-of, a bizarre quirk of this year's schedule, that this section has only ten students. I hope I don't screw it up.

Of course I do screw it up. I do this in two ways. First, I make the class way too easy. I think they have three papers per quarter or something. They write each one the night before in about half an hour. I just don't challenge them at all.

Second, I just let it get too chummy—there are so few of them, and they are easy kids to like—they are smart, they are funny, they like to write, and they talk in class. But it gets to the point where I have a hard time getting them to do anything because I've made them so comfortable in class that they don't feel like they have to really do the work. I give them a big lecture one day about how I'm not their friend. They look hurt and confused.

Strangely enough, we manage to overcome that crisis, and throughout most of the year the class goes smoothly. On parents' night I'm kind of embarrassed; all their parents come and tell me how grateful they are that their kid has my class, that they were really worried that their kid didn't do anything last year, all they did was watch movies.

Their teacher last year was a twenty-five-year veteran. Of course I am not above loving being told that I'm a better teacher than him, but it's also kind of embarrassing. I really shouldn't be better than him—he's got twenty-four years on me. And, to tell the truth, I'm not really that good yet. I mean, my heart's in the right place, and I work hard, and I believe that they should read and write in English class (most of the English faculty here share my point of view, but not all), but I am not half the teacher I am going to be and I am certainly not giving these kids enough work to prepare them for high-level college work. I make mistakes all the time.

One time I make a mistake by underreacting when a student writes a story about her committing suicide. I read it at home and fret all night, hoping she'll be alive the next morning when I get to work. She is, and I say to her, "Listen, Jeanie, I was really concerned by your story. Do you, um, you know, have somebody to talk to about this stuff?"

"Yes," she says curtly, and walks away. She later writes me a note about how terribly I overreacted, about how Stephen King writes lots of gory stories and nobody ever says that he has a problem (though given what he will later reveal about his alcohol and drug problems, all those stories of writers losing it maybe should have given us a clue that he did in fact have a problem, and I think *The Shining* is especially chilling when viewed in this light). I write her back that Stephen King doesn't write stories in which he is a character who kills himself, and that I was concerned because I care about her, blah blah blah, but I am intimidated by her anger and foolishly let it go at this, figuring, okay, somebody is on the case here. She lives to and beyond graduation, so my failure to follow up with parents, with the school psychologist, with anybody does not have fatal consequences. But the nice relationship we had been building—she is a good writer, I praise her good writing—evaporates, and she will barely speak to me for the next three years. Like Henry who cut himself, she can't forgive me for heeding her cry for help, though I never so much as mentioned it to another adult.

Despite alienating Jeanie and telling the kids I'm not their friend, I continue to have success in this class—I think it would be difficult not to with such a small group of motivated kids. So they write wonderful stuff, they say good things in discussions, and I don't succeed at all in creating any of the distance I was trying for in the "We're not friends" speech. This is okay, I guess, because one day I fart really loudly at a dead silent moment in class, and they don't mock me about it forever, at least not to my face, so I guess the excess chumminess does work in my favor at least this once.

Sometime after my attempted nonchummy crackdown, two of the students make a little cartoon poster of "Halpin's Funky Rules." It has a little cartoon of me saying things like, "Respect each other and listen while people talk." (Not really sure what's funky about that, but there you go.) I love it and post it in the room and refer to it frequently to remind them when one of the funky rules is being broken.

Then somebody draws a dick on the cartoon of me and I have to take it down.

In October, last year's twenty-five-year veteran who, according to my students and their parents, did nothing all year, is promoted to vice principal.

20

I **WILL HAVE** five different homerooms in my five years at Northton, thus guaranteeing that I will be unable to build any kind of relationship with any of the kids in my homeroom. It would take no effort at all for them to give me the same kids in homeroom every year. It must actually be more work to replace my name on their schedule with someone else's. Well, administrators work in strange ways.

One kid in my first-year homeroom, Chester, always refers to his math teacher, scornfully, as "Captain Jack."

I finally make the mistake of asking why he calls this guy, whose name is Eric, Captain Jack.

"'Cause he loves his Jack Daniel's! You know he's got a big old bottle in his closet that he hits between classes!"

I am appalled and I tell Chester that he has to stop slandering his math teacher with this name, that I don't like to hear him referring to him this way, that he has no kind of good information about this guy's drinking habits, that this is just kids starting malicious rumors.

He refuses to stop, or, more accurately, he seems unable to stop. We eventually reach a compromise whereby he refers to his math teacher as "the Captain."

I let it go, but I marvel at kids' ability to be malicious.

Then, at the end of the year, the Captain approaches me at about 10 A.M. because he is collecting money for the faculty end-of-the-year get-together, and he reeks of booze. The smell is pouring off of him like it does from the guys passed out on park benches, but he is not passed out on a park bench, he is gainfully employed as a high school math teacher.

Of course my first impulse is to go find Chester and apologize for doubting him. I don't, but I file this information away: kids always know.

21

SOMEHOW I GET conned into being the newspaper advisor. Like getting all the level-three classes, this is another initiation rite for new teachers—having all the crappy activities nobody else wants passed on to you. In this case, the newspaper is a hot potato because kids always want to write what they think and administrators always want to confiscate and/or burn such material.

I know absolutely nothing about putting a newspaper together, but they tell me that the kids know what to do, that I don't have to really do anything, and by the way, it's a twelve-hundred-dollar stipend. I am making more here than I did at Newcastle, but not so much that I can turn my nose up at twelve hundred bucks.

So I call an initial meeting, and probably fifty kids show up. By the time our second issue comes out, it's down to three. Two seniors run the thing, and they are ambitious, involved-in-everything-'cause-it-looks-good-on-my-college-application kind of kids, which is good because they are competent but bad because their energy is split fifty ways and they often have to neglect the newspaper in favor of one of their three sports teams or five other clubs.

One problem I can see immediately is that this paper is still laid out by hand. I seek out the district's computer guru, and, as such people always are, he is gruff and annoyed by mortals who don't understand his beloved technology or the terrible price he pays for loving it. He blows off my question about desktop publishing, and though the software exists in the building, he won't teach the kids how to use it or even take the ten minutes it would take to get us access to it so we can figure it out ourselves.

So this is my first big failing as a newspaper advisor. I give up at the first rejection. Later another new English teacher will come in and do the newspaper, and he will get computers with laser printers and desktop-publishing software installed in his room, which is pretty close to a loaves-and-fishes kind of miracle in a public school.

The kids put the paper together at a desultory pace. Around November we still have no product to show for my twelve-hundred-dollar stipend, and the *Northton Times* actually sends a reporter to interview me about what's taking so goddamned long to get the paper out. I have refused to take over or to really kick anybody's ass on this issue, figuring that my job is to advise a student activity, not actually perform the student activity. Apparently that was not the case. I'm glad I don't live in Northton, because I guess it would be embarrassing to make the paper for being a feeb, but I never so much as see the issue.

Eventually I get a call from a graduate of the school. She is a former editor who contracted a serious illness that took away her ability to walk, and she wants to help the kids put the paper together. Welcoming the help, I meet with her. She is a little bizarre, but she's in a wheelchair and she wants to help, and she does know her stuff.

Well, if I have been excessively hands-off, she is excessively hands-on. She comes to layout meetings and barks at the kids about how they are doing it all wrong, then attacks the page herself while the kids shoot me these looks like, "Who the hell is this and what the hell is wrong with her?"

Well, it quickly becomes clear that she wants this paper to be her project, and while I would probably welcome this because God knows the kids aren't really doing it, and I have to get something out to justify my stipend, the kids hate her. She just has no idea how to talk to them. Her tone ranges from gentle condescension to overt annoyance and abuse. Admittedly, this is also true of many teachers here at Northton High, but the kids *have* to put up with them, and they don't have to put up with her.

Finally the two coeditors come to me and beg me to fire her. I'm reluctant to do it because I am a coward, and because she is kind of pathetic, and I know that sounds awful but it's not because she's in a wheelchair but because she is thirty years old and seems to want nothing more than to put out a high school newspaper. Eventually they say that they'll quit the paper if I don't tell this woman to buzz off, and if these two quit, well, that's two thirds of the staff, and any illusions anybody has about this being a student product will be gone, and I'll probably make the front page of the *Northton Times* and give back the stipend, which I've already spent on plane tickets for my honeymoon.

So I make the call with my two editors standing there. I am way too cowardly to tell this woman that I don't like the way she treats the staff, so I just tell her that we have reached a decision that we really need to keep this thing in-house with only current students and faculty involved.

There is a terrible silence. I feel awful—clearly this was something this woman wanted to do to get back on her feet, figuratively speaking, following her illness, maybe test the waters for teaching or journalism or something, give something back to her alma mater, and I have taken it away from her. I feel like I've kicked a cripple, and I guess I kind of have.

She quickly assuages my guilt by getting abusive. She tells me that I don't know what I'm doing, that my staff doesn't know what they're doing. I don't argue. I know that taking the abuse is my part of the bargain.

She ends with "Your paper is going to be a piece of shit!"

Her vulgarity is completely unexpected because she's always been super prim around me and the kids, and it has the weird side effect of turning me into Cary Grant.

"Quite possibly true," I answer. "Good-bye."

Cassie and Jim, my staff, smile and give me the thumbs-up. We get one more issue out that year. As predicted, it is a piece of shit.

22

BECAUSE OF WHERE my classroom is in my first year, I don't get much contact with my colleagues. On one side of me is a hallway, and on the other is a rather grumpy old history teacher whose big welcome-to-the-neighborhood gesture to me is to open the connecting door and yell at my class when a kid from my room is passing notes under the door to a kid in his room. Across the hall are only science teachers. Everybody around me is at least twenty years older than I am. This makes for a kind of strange dynamic and probably explains why I let my sophomore class get too chummy—they are only eight years younger than I am and therefore are the closest thing I have to peers in this place.

Well, not quite. There is Lilly, a math teacher who is hired at the same time I am and who appears to be my age, yet for some reason we don't quite hit it off.

I go into the teachers' room once or twice to look over the local paper, but I quickly find that it's a horrible place where people do nothing but complain or talk about golf. Or sometimes complain about golf. They do get the paper delivered, so I go in to check the headlines once in a while, but I pretty much stop after the news breaks that a former Northton High student has been arrested for his role in a drive-by shooting in a neighboring town. The former student is black, one of the few black students this school has ever had, and some longtime teacher had gotten fired for saying to this kid, "I just can't stand some niggers." One history teacher, a guy who is sartorially stuck in the eighties—he wears a polo shirt under an oxford every single day—says, "Can you believe we had to lose a guy like Jim over this kid?"

A science teacher adds, "Well, with his coloration, at least he'll look good in prison orange." These are the worst two comments I hear, but the tone of everybody's conversation is pretty much the same: Jim was right, and some niggers just can't be stood.

Of course I have fantasies about standing up and denouncing the whole crew as a bunch of racists, but (also of course) I don't do it. Would I change their mind? Would they listen to someone as young as most of their children on this issue? What would I accomplish? I mean, you know, other than standing up for what's right. I wimp out, slink out, and thereafter visit the teachers' room only rarely, usually to microwave some leftovers.

But Lilly is in there every day. She hangs out and jokes with these guys and apparently even plays golf with them sometimes. Does she know that they talk about her (admittedly traffic-stopping) body in a less-than-completely-respectful-of-her-as-a-person way as soon as she leaves the room? I have to imagine she does—the woman works with sixteen-year-old boys and comes in wearing tight tops and short skirts every single day. I have no idea how boys in her class learn math. So either she knows that she's driving sixteen-year-old boys and fifty-five-year-old men nuts and kind of likes it, or she is completely clueless. In either case, she is able to fit into this world in a way that I just can't—that I don't want to.

One day in November I see her in the hall, and I say, "Are you happy here?" expecting to commiserate about how hard it is to work with a bunch of old people who don't really seem to like their jobs much, but she comes back with, "Yeah!" And I don't really know what to say.

Two young men are hired late, one because the twenty-five-year veteran is promoted to vice principal in October, and another because a science teacher—one of these midcareer professionals who changed from engineering to teaching, the kind of guy that everybody says the teaching profession needs to attract more of—proves so incompetent that he and the school mutually agree to part ways. This is a pretty spectacular achievement in a school where one science teacher is a notorious alcoholic (even more so than Captain Jack) who is apparently at least half in the bag all the time and one Spanish teacher suffers from some kind of mental illness that prompts him to spend entire class periods with his shoes propped up on his chest, sniffing them.

Anyway, I like these two new guys, but I never see them—none of us go to the teachers' room, so the only time I see them is at lunch. They spend every lunch period in the room of Andrew, an old, leathery English teacher who doesn't go to the teachers' room either. I join them a few times, but I quickly find Andrew tiresome—he pontificates a lot and tells the same stories over and over. He's only fifty, but he's kind of prematurely seventy. So I stop going down there and miss out on building much of a relationship with the new guys.

My feelings of isolation are alleviated somewhat by Terri, Tim's wife, who got me the interview here. I really like her, and one day I mention to her very casually that I really want my students to start doing some kind of writing portfolio, but I just can't figure out the logistics and grading, and she says to me, "You'll never try anything new if you wait until you have it totally figured out. Just jump in and see what happens!" This is probably the single best piece of teaching advice I ever get, and it really sets me on the road to being a better teacher. But Terri and I are on different floors and have different lunch periods, so I very rarely see her.

At the end of the year the principal retires—two of his last acts are to finally gather the necessary documentation to get rid of the drunk and the shoe sniffer. I feel like I have to go to the retirement dinner, and it is horrible. Terri is talking to people she's known for thirty years, and I end up sitting at a table with some young people who are nice, but for some reason I just don't feel like I fit in. I'm always most comfortable when I'm the most normal person in the group, and here—I am a vegetarian, I live in the city, I like punk rock, I was not in a fraternity in college—I am by far the weirdest. The event is kind of psychotic too. Due to events at least ten years in the past, approximately half the faculty hates this guy's guts. But everybody shows up at the retirement dinner, and people say insincere things about how great he is. (I haven't really known him long enough to form much of an opinion. He fired two incompetent teachers in a year, which is a pretty significant achievement, but he waited years to do it—some of my students' parents talk about the science teacher having vodka bottles in his desk back when *they* were students.)

When I get a little older I will understand that there is a lot of class in what happens here—not in the awful food or the atmosphere or anything, but the man was a principal here for decades, and sending him off with a tacky catered affair is the right thing to do, and, to their credit, these people do it no matter how they feel about him.

This is hard for me to understand at age twenty-four, though. I feel like a dork for not fitting in at my table, I hate the insincerity of the whole thing, and I am depressed that I work at a place where I feel so alone.

I get in my car, pop in the punk mix that my friend Karl made for me in the eleventh grade, turn up Stiff Little Fingers, and go home.

23

IN MY SECOND year at Northton High I am assigned a new classroom. It is in what turns out to be a really sweet location—a dead end of the hallway with three classrooms on only one side. Next to my classroom is one occupied by a science teacher, the kind

of teacher that people call Coach. He sometimes teases male students he likes by calling them "faggot," and he unironically displays
a sign in his classroom that says, ATTITUDES ARE CONTAGIOUS! IS
YOURS WORTH CATCHING?

Through the connecting door from me is Andrew, the old guy I
hated eating lunch with last year. The two younger guys I liked are
gone—one transferred to the middle school, while the other went
to a school fifty miles away—but there is precedent for me eating in
Andrew's room, and so sort of by default, he and I end up having
lunch together every day. I have stopped going to the teachers'
room even to microwave my lunch, because the walk up to the third
floor and the three minutes of heating time take precious time out
of my allotted twenty-three minutes.

Andrew and I don't have a lot in common apart from the fact that
we both hate the teachers' room. Basically he likes to hold forth on
stuff, and I listen. It starts to kind of suck, as I knew it would after
my experience last year, but I don't know how to stop. He will stick
his head through the connecting door and say, "Lunch?" I can't very
well say, "No, actually I prefer to sit in here and eat by myself."

He's really not a bad guy, it's just that we are from different
worlds, we think different things are important. For example, he
seems to really value propriety, whereas I rarely give a shit about it.
Sometimes this concern with propriety has made him do good
things—he frequently tells the story of dropping a dime on the
school to the local papers when there was some kind of stunt involving watermelons at a pep rally before Northton played a predominately black high school. But he talks very nastily about a
certain segment of his students—the gum-chewing, blue-collar
girls who seem to offend him because they speak their minds at
somewhat inappropriate times. (I tend to love kids like this.) He
does this terrible impression of this one girl, who, okay, once dis-
rupted his class by washing her feet in the sink in the back of the
room, and he occasionally refers to these girls as "bitches," and by

the end of the year, when he's really coming apart at the seams, his epithets grow much more colorful.

And I still can't get out of it. I disagree with him twice, and it pisses him off mightily. One time he has this really cute student teacher, and the three of us are having lunch, and some educational thing comes up, and I make the mistake of getting into it (he doesn't have his students do any writing, so there's just not a whole lot of common ground here). I disagree with him in front of her, and the student teacher kind of agrees with me, and he gives me the cold shoulder for a couple of days.

Later, at a meeting, our boss goes off on how she just wants to go home, can we please come to an agreement here, and he says to me the next day, "That was a real example of female high dudgeon last night." Tired of his misogyny, I say, "Well, you've kinda got a thing about that female thing, huh?"

He gets mad and tells me to grow up. This somehow infuriates me, and I yell back at him, "Don't you tell me to grow up!" Later we both apologize and continue to have lunch together.

It's a complicated relationship. He drives me nuts, he tells the same stories over and over again, and yet sometimes he is very funny, and I feel sorry for him in a way—he seems to be deeply sad. He is also a heavy smoker, and since Northton, like all schools in Massachusetts, is required by state law to have a smoke-free campus, he can't go to the lounge and smoke anymore, so he sneaks into the men's room to smoke, and when you're sixteen, I guess smokin' in the boys room is cool enough to write a song about, but when you're fifty, it's just kind of sad. (It also makes it kind of horrible to go pee because the bathroom is usually fogged with cigarette smoke.)

At the end of the year the administration decides they want to break up the gang of burnouts who all have lunch together and hang out in the teachers' room, turning it into a black hole of negativity, and so they move several people's rooms. They invent this cool cover story about how this will "allow for interdisciplinary work," and they try to move history teachers next to English teachers and math teachers next to science teachers. Griping and golf are about the only interdisciplinary activities that ever go on here, but what the hell—I guess they feel like the truth is too ugly.

Anyway, though I am not a burnout they're trying to keep out of the teachers' room, I do get my room moved—all the way up to the third floor. Everybody else is running around all pissed off, but I am relieved. It's the only way I could ever get out of these lunches.

24

I HAVE A CLASS of juniors this year that proves to be the biggest failure of my entire career. I also lose this class on the first day, but at least this time I don't think it's my fault. There is a girl in the class named Jaime, but a misprint on my little class sheet lists her sex as M, so I assume that this is one of our five Hispanic students and that his name is pronounced "Hi-may."

Well, this just about paralyzes this group, they think I am the stupidest dork ever to walk the earth, and it will be nearly impossible to get any work out of them for the rest of the year. Partially this is just bad chemistry. Among the students is William, who is actually a senior and who spends a lot of time just being bizarre, including one day very early on when I look over and he has the window shade tied around his ear and is coloring his tongue with a green Magic Marker.

I also have Shawna, who is prone to adding non sequiturs to class discussion, who never does any work, who is inexplicably a junior in high school despite the fact that she has passed a total of one class in her first two years here. My efforts to get her removed from the class simply because she doesn't have the credits to be a junior get

nowhere, either because her guidance counselor is a twisted fuck
who hates me or because to demote her would create difficulties
schoolwide regarding kids who are inappropriately placed. Probably both are true.

I talk to Shawna in the hall privately after she disrupts class almost every day. Most kids, with the notable exception of Jimmy last
year, can have decent conversations in the hall away from an audience, but not Shawna. She shuffles her feet and mumbles, "Aw, iss
all good, G" (I should point out that Shawna is white) and other
things she seems to have heard in movies or songs. Having a conversation with her is a strange, frustrating experience—only very
rarely do her contributions seem to match up in any way with anything I am asking her or telling her.

Finally I go to the school psychologist. "Oh, yeah," he says,
"Shawna has got some serious problems. I really think she'll probably be institutionalized by the time she's twenty." Which of course
implies that we really can't educate her here, which one might have
concluded from the fact that she's failed everything she's ever taken
except for one semester of gym, and which means that the school
psychologist should really make strong recommendations to get this
kid into a residential program or something, but of course he won't
do that, because if the district admits that it can't serve a kid like
this, then they have to kick in for her education in some kind of
therapeutic setting. Which they can't afford to do. So Shawna stays,
and fails my class and every other class. The next year she will make
a stab at being a senior, though she is still technically a freshman,
but she will drop out about halfway through the year. Problem
solved.

And there is King, who appears to really be named King because
that is the name on all official school documents referring to him
and who engages in jolly pranks like coloring a tampon with a red
marker and tossing it into the middle of the room while my back is
turned.

I have various meetings with King and his parents, but not much ever changes. The tampon thing is the most egregious example, but he will torture me like this all year. Still, I have it easy compared to the sub who comes in when the district makes me go to some mandatory training thing for the phoney-baloney "initiative" they are doing. I spend three days with a couple of other young teachers and a bunch of burnouts (this is the mandatory indoctrination for people who have missed the voluntary sessions) listening to this improbably tight-panted guy from North Carolina tell us stupid jargony names for stuff we already do. Now they can say their entire staff has been trained in the Tight-Panted Southerner Education System! And the only impact it has or will ever have in anybody's classroom is that a bunch of kids got an even more half-assed education than usual around here because they were going nuts with substitutes.

When I get back to my classes after three days, it takes a while to reestablish any kind of momentum, especially in period four, where apparently it has been a free-for-all. Kids tell me in whispers about the sub screaming obscenities at them, about King making a blowtorch out of a can of graffiti-remover spray he found in the closet. Nobody tells me how my coffee mug got broken or who covered the entire rear wall of the classroom with liquid soap.

This is in November, and while it never gets as bad as this again, it also never gets to the point where I feel like I'm getting anything done with this class. A few days later, one of my students bails and switches classes. They are not supposed to be allowed to do this, but it happens all the time. She comes to me to break the news. "I'm going to Mr. Black's class," she says. "No offense, but your class is a joke."

Well. None taken.

One of my colleagues tells me he thinks I'm being too experimental with them (because I give them photocopies of Walt Whitman poems that are not in the anthology) and I should just do what he does, which is go through every story, essay, and poem in the anthology and have the kids answer the questions at the end, and give them a multiple-choice test every two weeks. In other words, bore them into submission.

Of course I scorn this advice, but it couldn't really have been much worse than what I did. At the end of the year, one of the parents of a kid who goes along with the crowd, which means he would have done well in a class with some order but acted like a jackass in this class, comes to talk to me about the class.

"Why do you think this happened?" she asks me, and not in a hostile way. It's not like she's blaming me (though she could)—more like she's trying to help me, which in some way makes me feel worse.

"I don't know," I say. "Maybe it's just the mix of kids, or maybe I failed to do something in September that would have made things different. Whatever it is, I feel horrible, because this is their only chance at junior English, and now it's over and it was less than it could have been, and I can teach this class next year and try to get it right, but this is the only junior English they'll ever have."

True. If you believe your job is important, then fucking up is especially painful.

Then again, maybe I overestimate my importance. Six years later I will run into King. We have a nice conversation—he seems happy to see me, and I enjoy talking to him. I always liked him in spite of the fact that he tortured me—he's smart and very funny. He is in college, and he is succeeding despite learning little else but tampon coloring in his junior English class. He says he runs an "entertainment management business" on the side.

We are both adults now, so I say, "What's that, King—porno?"

He smiles and laughs. "Naw, naw, we coordinate deejays for parties, a few bands . . . well, okay, and a couple of strippers too."

25

M Y NINTH-GRADE CLASS this year is much like last year's classes—some good stuff happens and some bad stuff happens. It is notable for two things. One is that after the first quarter, the class gets a Hispanic kid from a neighboring town. He is the second Hispanic kid to enter the school since Kent beat the shit out of that kid last year. I take to him immediately, because he's funny and smart, even if he doesn't really do any work.

But the other kids ostracize him immediately. Given what happened last year with Kent and Snoop Dogg, I immediately decide that these kids, though I like them, are just ignorant and prejudiced and can't get along with someone different. I am annoyed with them for their bigotry.

Two years later I will have some of these same kids in my writing class, and when I bring this up, they protest: "That kid was a jerk! He offered to sell me coke in the bathroom on the first day he was in school!" So maybe I misjudged them.

This class gives me my first big revelation about discipline. I have a bit of trouble with Mark and Peter throwing stuff at each other. Actually, they do it every day. Mostly it's erasers that they break off of their pencils, which is at least preferable to spitballs, which make a terrible mess. So one day I turn around quickly from the board and find both Mark and Peter right in the act of cocking their arms with erasers aimed at each other, and I say, "Okay guys, you have detention," because this is my big punishment and the schoolwide discipline policy. I start filling out the slips and Peter gives a completely nonchalant "Okay" and throws the eraser anyway.

And I realize from his tone of voice and the expression on his face that this is not a fuck-you gesture aimed at me; it's a "here comes the eraser" gesture aimed at his buddy. Peter, in fact, doesn't care if he has detention. Peter pretty much has detention every day, and so it's not really a punishment to him. In fact, Peter's no dummy—he's figured out that if he just budgets an extra hour into every day (and why not? What else does he have to do?), he can, within reason, do pretty much anything he wants during the school day including, but not limited to, pegging his buddy with an eraser.

It's the last time I give detention.

I also have a sophomore class this year that proves to be one of the best I ever have. About two thirds of the students in this class were my students last year as ninth-graders, so we totally hit the ground running—it is amazing to me how much more work this class gets done than any of my others just because we don't have to spend the first quarter getting to know each other.

One day, after reading Alice Walker's "Everyday Use," which is about, among other things, tradition and sibling rivalry, we have a fantastic conversation not unlike the "We Are Seven" class. In this discussion, the class uses the smart, ugly narrator's decision to give the quilts to the dumb, ugly daughter instead of the smart, beautiful one as a springboard to talking about their own problems with their siblings and their insecurity about which sibling their parents prefer. As my juniors at Newcastle did, these kids keep looping back and forth between the story and their lives. Once again I have stumbled into forty-five minutes of greatness. I am less satisfied this time, though, because while with the Newcastle juniors just getting them to talk about a poem passionately seemed like a real accomplishment, now I feel like I want to be able to take this somewhere, to build on this discussion and make it mean something beyond just that we had a good class today. I don't, but I do think everybody realizes that something special happened, and even if it doesn't lead anywhere concrete, it does lend a positive tone to the class that is sustained throughout the year. I don't really remember many other specifics: I take them to see *The Glass Menagerie* at a local theater, and they are amazingly good; I turn around one day and see Chester, the kid from my homeroom, doing some kind of doggie-style pantomime and spanking his own ass, and I have to pretend I had no idea what he was doing; and I mistakenly give Denise a detention one day because she tells Chester loudly that he's an asshole because he is, in fact, being an asshole to her. (After class she tells me the whole story, teary-eyed, and I tell her to forget about the detention, that I screwed up. When I stop giving detentions, I won't have these kind of problems.) Mike periodically torments Max, who is such a *Star Trek* fan that he's taught himself to speak Klingon, by saying, "Max is a Trekkie!" and Max takes the bait every time, replying indignantly, "Trek*ker*! Trek*ker*!"

At the end of the year I write this class a good-bye letter and tell them that they are the best class I have ever had. It's true, despite the fact that we had one day out of 180 that was fantastic. Most days are not fantastic, but almost every day is functional and productive, and at the end of it, I feel proud of what's happened during that forty-five minutes.

I am in my third year as a teacher, and for the first time, I feel like I'm getting good at it.

26

A T THE END of this year, I get on the committee that's going to hire three new English teachers—because our enrollment is going way up, not because anyone is leaving. This is so cool! I'm really excited about it, and Terri kind of takes charge and says all seven of us want to see all the résumés instead of having the clowns in the central office sort through them for us, so we all do this, and it takes forever (if you whisper the words "job opening" and "English teacher" to yourself in a locked room, you will probably find five or six résumés being slipped under the door), but it's kind of fun.

Well, except for the fact that some of these résumés came from some job fair where people had some pre-interview. Our moron superintendent wrote "bright and beautiful" on one woman's interview sheet. There is a student on the committee, and I am embarrassed for the school that she sees this, but I'm also just appalled—this guy is supposed to be running the joint, and he doesn't have the good sense not to write a blatantly illegal comment on a sheet that's going to be circulated to at least seven people including a student.

I complain to my department head and principal, and they both tell me to relax, he didn't really mean anything by it, that's just the kind of thing he says—but I do notice that the sheet with the "bright and beautiful" comment disappears from the stack.

They make us give her an interview, though she didn't make the cut from anybody on the committee. She is sort of generically cute but certainly not what I'd call beautiful; however, she's a lot closer to beautiful than bright. She gives these Miss America answers to all the interview questions. If you ask her if she prefers A or B, she replies, "Well, on the one hand, I really believe in A, but of course I also firmly believe in B, though they are polar opposites and mutually exclusive."

Rrgh. Fortunately they don't make us hire her.

The only other kind of weird thing that happens is that some of the older teachers on the committee start getting their insecurities a little ruffled by the process. We don't consider people with more than a year or two of experience—this is a budget thing—and there are so many résumés from people with really top-notch schools on them that we don't even really consider people from the local public college that about half the staff here attended. So this just adds pain to what is, under the best of circumstances, a painful process. (After all, we're trying to get seven people—six of whom are teachers and therefore talkative know-it-alls—to agree on something. Three times.)

After many long, agonizing days of interviewing and arguing, we end up getting three really great people, and I'm excited, even though one of them is devastatingly handsome, has all these great new ideas, and is a published freelance writer. He is in every way cooler than me, so, like thick-calved Nancy back at Newcastle High, I am about to lose my identity as "the Young, Cool One." Now I'll be "kind of like an uglier, crankier version of Mr. Paulsen." Oh, well.

I begin my third year at Northton feeling hopeful. Three new English teachers! Three colleagues close to my age!

Unfortunately, I find out that Kurt and Jesse are on the second floor in adjoining rooms, while I am on the third floor with a history teacher on one side and the boys' bathroom on the other. This is fine—the history teacher terrorizes the students, but they love him for it; he's one of those "I bust your ass because I care" guys, and the kids get it and love him. He also has a very dry sense of humor, which it usually takes the kids several months to tune into. The boys' room is fine—because it's close, I usually end up using it, and my presence there probably causes, in total, several cartons of cigarettes to be dumped into toilet bowls or thrown out the window. The battle I have about the boys' room is the soap. Weeks will go by where there's none, and eventually the empty dispenser is ripped off the wall, and then we get a new soap dispenser, and then it's ripped off the wall while it's still full. The whole thing is strangely depressing. Eventually I just bring my own soap. Sometimes I will leave it in the bathroom. And then it gets thrown out.

I'm feeling jealous of Kurt and Jesse downstairs. I do have Caroline, the third new teacher, on this floor for two periods a day—she is "floating" room to room like I did my first year at Newcastle—but she is way down the hall with the math teachers. Caroline and I do get to be friends, but my dreams of a little new-teacher community evaporate almost immediately. I just don't have any incidental contact with Kurt and Jesse; somebody has to go make the effort to go see somebody else, and I do end up going down there from time to time, and it's nice, but it's always me going down there—they never come up to see me because they have each other—and that gets kind of old.

Maybe they also don't come up to see me because the majority of the English teachers are up here, and the new kids are not exactly welcomed with open arms. This is largely a reflection of the fact that the staff here hates the administration, and the English department in particular really hates the English-department head because . . . well, because she is in charge of English K–12 in this system, and she's never really been an English teacher. She was some kind of elementary-school gifted-and-talented teacher. So while I am not particularly insulted by being evaluated by this woman—I still feel insecure enough to feel like almost anybody knows more about teaching than I do—the people who have been doing this for twenty-plus years really resent this and, as a result, hate her.

Also she's just too nice. She tries to be kind to everybody, and as students will do to a teacher like this, our department just eats her alive because she wants so badly to be liked, and while I do like her most of my colleagues hate her with a venom people usually reserve for people who sleep with their spouse or kill their dog, so she should just give up trying, but she can't. Some of these old fuckers are just tough as nails, and they chew her up. (She cries in and after department meetings on what seems like a regular basis but is probably really just twice.)

So the new teachers are automatically suspect because they come from fancy-shmancy schools, they are hired by the new administration, and they seem to embody all the grievances that the old teachers have about having been disrespected by an evil or possibly just very stupid administration for twenty years.

The department head totally plays into this by having the new teachers make a presentation to the department about Socratic seminars, which is education-speak for students running the discussion instead of teachers, and the old people instantly mock the idea. (I think the idea is cool and try it out; it works great for me except for the part about assigning kids roles—"You are the recorder!" "You are the discussion-mover-alonger!"—which always feels corny and artificial.) But the "veterans" just can't even be courteous about it, and it becomes a running joke to a few of them in future meetings. So this is our department head screwing up by making it seem like the new kids are here to teach the old people, but the irony is that she probably could have never gotten any of the old folks to talk to the department about teaching, and if she had, nobody would have listened. Teaching is the one thing that we never talk about here. I guess after doing something in isolation for twenty years, you don't want to think that you might have been doing it wrong. One guy, who is long-winded and cranky but at least intelligent and articulate, even explains how he feels implicitly disrespected by all the fuss being made over new people, because what the hell, he's been doing this for twenty-five years and wouldn't mind a little fuss over everything he's achieved. He is right and I respect him for it even though he develops a pretty pathological hatred of me as the symbol of this whole thing.

So the old people are, if anything, more hostile than ever, and no wonderful new teacher collaborative has developed.

But it's kind of okay, because this year my classes suddenly start to get much better, which makes the new teacher collaborative feel less desperately important than it did before, when I just really needed to know that I wasn't the only one fucking up all the time.

Of course, I'm still fucking up all the time, but, as I said, it's starting to get better. I am on my third round of teaching ninth-graders, so while their behavior continues to vex me, I am no longer tossing textbooks across the room, and now I at least have a pretty good idea of what I do in what order and the confidence to make the class harder than it used to be. But still probably not *hard*, like the history teacher next door. Though I do aspire to be the guy that everybody hates and then loves because he's so tough, I pretty much have to accept that it's never going to happen.

For the first time, I have an all-writing elective. The school has switched from year-long forty-five-minute classes to semester-long ninety-minute classes, and this has opened some holes in the schedule, so I create this writing-workshop class.

Initially, it's not that popular. My first class has three students. While this earns me the wrath of the twisted guidance counselor who hates me (on the couple of occasions when I am forced to have a conversation with him and I mention the class, he says, "Oh, the one that the school committee is so concerned about? The one they want to shut down? That one?"), and it sometimes gets kind of claustrophobic, we end up doing much more work on writing than I would have believed possible in a school situation.

Of course, I need more students if the class is going to continue. One of the three initial students is an originator of the "funky rules," and this trend will continue: every time I teach this class, at least a third of the students will be kids I've taught before. I am too insecure at the time to realize what a powerful endorsement this is, but in later years it will strike me as a really nice compliment that I should have appreciated more.

My number comes up in the scheduling lottery or something, because I also get some of the coveted level-one classes. Well, this also happens to be because the do-nothing veteran who had taught my funky-rules kids as ninth-graders got demoted back to English teacher when the new principal came in, and he requested all level-three classes, because he realized that as long as you keep those kids quiet, nobody really cares if they don't do any work, and he was, to his credit, very skilled at keeping them quiet, which is something I never mastered.

Anyway, I have a level-one class, and while I do have some struggles, I don't have to deal with a lot of behavior problems. Which is good, because I still suck at that. I am now having after-school "meet-

ings" with kids rather than giving them detentions—they fill out a
form about what's been happening, and we talk about it for a few
minutes, and it is sort of effective in that most kids would rather be
yelled at than be called on to examine and explain their behavior—it
just makes them squirm—but I don't follow through very well, and
my classes are still more chaotic than I'd like.

The kids in this class do their homework, they participate, they
are great. Their papers kind of suck, though, mostly because they
are long on opinions and short on evidence to back them up, but
also because most of them seem to have been taught that you need
to say the exact same thing in your introduction and conclusion,
presumably to make your reader say uncle and submit to your argument, if only to stop you saying "Macbeth's tragic flaw is ambition" over and over and over. I give them an opportunity to rewrite
them, but most kids don't do it. So after one quarter I stop giving
grades. I am convinced that the department or the parents or
somebody will give me hell about this, but strangely, nobody does.
I tell the kids that I will grade the entirety of their work at the end
of the quarter, and until then, I will just make comments on their
papers.

This has the strange effect of making them do multiple drafts,
which is something I've always struggled with. While they wouldn't
bother to rewrite a paper with a C on it, they will happily rewrite
papers again and again until they get a comment from me that says,
"Everything looks great! You're done!" It ends up being a smashing
success, and though the kids kind of hate me for it at the time, they
do fantastic work. It remains to be seen whether they will love me
for it later, but at least I've finally achieved half of my dream of
being a hated-then-loved hard-ass.

I think I've finally found it—the educational Holy Grail! The success gives me some confidence I've never had before. This class is
really hard, and the kids rise to the challenge and do great work,
and I guess that must mean I am a good teacher.

I like to think that this is due to my great idea about the grades, and that this is a vindication of my whole philosophy, but in fact the no-grades approach works well next year with level-one sopho-mores but fails horribly with level-three freshmen. I can tell you all the reasons why this is the best way to do things, but the fact is that it doesn't always work. So when it works, am I skilled or just lucky?

27

I'M BEGINNING TO FIND my place at Northton High. By my fourth year, there are no students here who remember the school without me in it, so I am sort of an institution. One of my students makes a sign for my room that says WELCOME TO ROOM 206: HOME OF THE HALPINATOR. My writing-workshop class gets more popu-lar, and I end up teaching two sections per semester. My teaching is getting less memorable. I mean this in an entirely good way—I still have some fantastic classes now and again, and I meet some really interesting and definitely memorable kids who write some wonder-ful things for me, we have good discussions, but now I've gotten good enough at this that I can continue to do a decent job even in the sleep-deprived fog of new parenthood, and it's no longer a big event when a class goes well. (Though it's still an event when it goes spectacularly well.) And I've had enough bad classes that a bad day no longer seems like the end of the world. There are still times at the end of the day when I sit at my desk and I would put my head down on it in despair if it weren't for the fact that it's covered in crap and there's no room for my head, but for the most part I am in the groove here.

While my work with the kids is getting better and better, my col-leagues remain a pretty constant irritant. I tend to leave faculty meetings grinding my teeth, both because they are so deadly boring and because most of the staff seems to live just for the bitter joy of scorning anything new or any kind of meaningful talk about education at all. Many, many meetings degenerate into someone holding forth on the importance of the hat rule. Students at Northton are not allowed to wear hats in school, and so we periodically revisit this issue, with one of the vice principals reminding us of the importance of uniform enforcement of the rule and some old teacher complaining about kids today, no respect, can't even see their eyes with those damn things on. Once I make the mistake of saying that the kids really don't understand this rule, that they generally obey rules that they understand (audible snorts from the cranky old people at that assertion), and that they continually break this rule because it seems arbitrary to them, and if we could just explain it, we might have better compliance. I am shouted down by a history teacher who yells, "It's about RESPECT!" thereby ending the discussion without actually saying anything.

So we can talk all day about the hat rule, or the new detention slips, or any of the logistics of controlling the student population, but we can't possibly talk about teaching, except in ones and twos behind closed doors. It just depresses the hell out of me that so much of our collective energy is focused on stupid bullshit that has very little to do with what we're doing here, and there is just no energy or passion for talking about working with kids.

This becomes especially painful when the New England Association of Schools and Colleges is scheduled to come for our evaluation visit, and the English department has to assemble some kind of curriculum to show them. After one contentious meeting in which I say that I hate *The Old Man and the Sea* because I do hate it, but also because I know that an old English teacher who hates me is a Hemingway cultist and that statement is sure to infuriate him, we all break into groups and spend hours and hours crafting documents that are worded so vaguely as to allow us all to continue doing exactly what we've always done.

Still, we have only one faculty meeting a month and one department meeting a month, and, thanks to the good offices of our
union, we get to get right up and walk out at the contractual ending
time even if (and, for some people I think it's especially if) the principal is in the middle of a sentence, so I have only two afternoons a
month and the occasional all-day training in which to think about
this. Most of the time I spend with kids, and that time is very good.

I do, however, have a couple of unpleasant encounters with parents. Up to now, I haven't had much parental contact—I've talked
to them at parents' night, I think an attractive single mom hit on me
once, though I'm not really sure, and some of them have given me
nice letters or cards of thanks for the work I've done with their kids.
These are hugely valuable because they are about the only real and
informed praise I've ever gotten from grown-ups. I appreciate it
when the three colleagues I can stand to talk to tell me I'm doing a
good job, but they never actually see me teach. My supervisor has
never seen me teach more than three class periods in an entire year,
which doesn't seem to me to be enough to make any kind of judgment. But the parents at least have heard what their kids say when
they say what they really think, and maybe they've even got some
basis for comparison, so praise from them means a lot.

But this year I have Jeff. Jeff's older brother, Elvis, is a star student and headed to Harvard next fall. Jeff, though, is a less than
stellar student who is happy to play football well and really has no
desire to go to Harvard.

Unfortunately for both of us, Jeff's mom is not having this. So we
end up having just endless meetings in which she asks me pointedly
how it could be that Jeff has a C in my class, and I answer that, well,
he never does his homework, and then she says how she has a really
hard time with him on that issue but then again implies that I am
doing something really wrong, and this is reflected in the fact that
Jeff isn't doing his homework. We have this conversation at least
four times, but it feels like forty, and Jeff's mom's point veers wildly

between "Why is Jeff fucking up, why can't he get his act together?" and "If only you were a competent teacher, Jeff would be getting good grades like his brother." It's exhausting, irritating, and, by the fourth iteration, boring.

My writing workshop this year includes, along with former students of mine who love to write, a number of kids who did not request it but were placed in it to fill a hole in their schedule. This makes for an odd mix. One schedule-filler is a senior who comes into the class every day and places his head on the desk and goes to sleep. He literally does nothing. At the end of the year I fail him, and he apparently needed the credits from this class to graduate, and so his parents make an issue. The twisted-asshole guidance counselor who hates everybody but seems particularly dedicated to being my personal nemesis is practically licking his lips as he tells me that I have to prove I warned the kid's parents that he was going to fail. I am incredulous. I ask if the student will have to prove he did any work. The guidance counselor walks away rubbing his hands together in delight like a villain in a silent movie. At least that's how I remember it. Then again, I also remember him in full Snidely Whiplash regalia during this conversation, so my memory may be playing tricks here.

Miraculously I find copies of the warning slips in the pile of crap that covers my desk. I give them to the principal and never hear anything further about it. Apparently the parents continue to make a stink because somehow the necessary credits suddenly appear on the student's transcript. It's a strange and miraculous occurrence. One day he can't graduate without credits from my class, the next he is buying his cap and gown. Go figure.

Other than these two encounters, though, I don't see much of the parents and, as I said, my classes generally go pretty well. Caroline has stopped "floating" and now has a classroom on the third floor, so we see each other a lot and actually talk about teaching, and it just helps enormously. This is probably another reason why I feel like I'm in the groove here—I finally have regular contact with someone with a similar philosophy who I can talk to about what's happening in our classes. I also have somebody to sit next to at our insufferable faculty meetings.

I have my first level-three class in four years. Like my most difficult class at Newcastle, this is a ninth-grade group composed almost entirely of special-ed students. Unlike that class, this one actually does something, and I guess this, as much as anything, is a measure of how far I've come in five years of teaching. My big success is that I get most of them to read *Ender's Game,* a four-hundred-page science fiction novel about a misfit kid who makes good. The kids love it. Many of them tell me it's the first book they have ever finished. Certainly it is the longest book any of them have ever read.

Not that it's an easy class. My "no grades till the end of the quarter" thing flops horribly here. They still do only one draft of a paper, if that, but with these kids the behavioral stuff is much more important than the academic stuff. Particularly difficult are the two Bretts. One is thin, one is fat, and both are loud and out of control a lot, though they are both good-natured and I like them. Both can stop the class dead and do so about three times per period.

On the third-to-last day of class I completely lose it with fat Brett. He is saying something, I can't remember what it is, but he just keeps saying it over and over, and I ask him nicely to stop, and he won't, and finally I just lose my mind. I get right in his face and scream, "Shut up! Will you just shut up!" He looks at me like I just hit him. I wonder if he might be used to this kind of treatment. The other kids laugh. The next day I apologize to him. I will feel guilty for years about this.

On the last day of school, thin Brett is one of only two kids who bother to come. He has to come because he got suspended last week and was required by the vice principal to attend the last three days of school as a condition of his punishment. If he blows off school today, he'll have to go to summer school.

So here he is, early even, but he is untouchable. Grades are already in, and there is no detention tomorrow; the only possible punishment he could get today is to be arrested for something. So he runs into the hall and eventually finds a wheeled garbage can that kids have been using when they clean out their lockers.

He gets a running start, then flops on top of the can, arms out, and rides it down the long hallway. For about ten minutes I feebly tell him he has to stop. Come on, Brett, please, really, it's not safe, hey, come back here. Eventually I just give up. Later he discovers the handicapped-accessible ramps and spends the rest of the day going "Whee!" and flying down the ramps atop a garbage can. It's probably the best day of school he will ever have.

28

EVEN THOUGH THINGS are going well in most respects, I am not happy here. At the end of my fourth year both Kurt and Jesse leave Northton High. They both live far away and so have good reasons to leave, but the bottom line is that this is just not a place where they can see themselves staying.

I feel the same way. In fact, I've always felt the same way, which is why I always send out résumés in the spring. In fact, while I've gotten better and better at working with the kids, and I even handled the two pain-in-the-ass parents okay, the other teachers here are driving me nuts. I have started to just really hate them. It gets to the point where I write a thinly veiled attack on them that I actually read to one of my writing-workshop classes. I call two of my colleagues "weasel boy" and "the eggman" in this masterpiece.

So it is October of my fifth year at Northton High. I have two very high-energy classes of sophomores who talk about getting drunk all the time, but I don't really feel like it's anything I can't handle. I have what may be the best writing-workshop class ever. And yet . . .

I can't sleep. Every night I lie down, tired to the bone, and I can't fall asleep. It's like I have forgotten how to fall asleep. I lie awake for hours. Sometimes I get up and watch TV. Once I see the Ben Folds Five on Conan O'Brien and there are only three of them, and they rock, and, like the old men when I was a kid who thought Molly Hatchet sure had a deep voice for a girl, I thought they were a five-piece piano pop band, and here they are rocking with guitars on late-night TV. I question whether there is even a guy named Ben Folds in the band. Probably not. Am I dreaming this?

If only. I won't dream anything until I finally fall asleep. Usually this is somewhere between two and four in the morning. I get up at quarter to six.

I go to the doctor. He gives me a prescription for Ambien. I take one and sleep for six hours in a row, though I wake up feeling not very refreshed. I am too familiar with both *Valley of the Dolls* and the life of Elvis Presley to be really comfortable taking a pill to fall asleep. I take it one other time, then flush the rest of the bottle down the toilet.

I go to a therapist. We have some nice talks. He tells me I need to get a book on "sleep hygiene." I don't.

I go to a homeopathic doctor. He gives me a dose of sulphur, or rather of lactose powder, which once touched something that touched something that touched a molecule of sulphur.

Friday nights I sleep fine. Saturday nights I sleep fine. Sundays I can't sleep, and won't sleep again until Friday. The same thing happens every weekend. It doesn't take a genius to figure out that this has something to do with work. So what is it? Well, fortunately, I have a lot of time to think about it. Here is what I come up with.

I have done okay at Northton. Actually I have done better than okay. I have gone from a second-year teacher who knew nothing to a sixth-year teacher who is, mostly, very good at his job. My classes used to be easy—now I do actually bust kids' butts sometimes. I created a writing elective. I love my students and have been really lucky to build some nice relationships with a lot of them.

And yet Northton is a totally white suburb of Boston. I am spending two hours a day to get there. I now have a nine-month-old daughter, and time is getting more and more precious. I feel strangely disconnected, like I am disintegrating. I'm hopping between two cultures. At home, I live in this diverse neighborhood (though we liberal white folks who like to crow about this never talk about how, for the most part, it is carefully segregated street by street. So when we say we really value the diversity, we mean we see people browner than us at the supermarket, but very few of us live on the same street or in the same building as them). I am part of the city, I want to make the city a better place, and yet I am using the only skills I have to do that twenty-six miles away. I meant it when I said I belonged in the city, but I couldn't get a job there, and I got one here, and working in the city was the reason I got into this, and after five years, I feel like my dream is slipping out of my reach.

My students come from a culture that is getting more and more foreign to me. Yes, we are all white, and yes, economically I have a lot in common with many of them. But I have never lived this kind of life, never lived in the world of basement rec rooms and hanging at the mall, and every day when I drive through the long rows of identical ranch houses to get to work, I think to myself, what the hell am I doing here? Some of my students laugh openly when I mention the neighborhood I live in. Many more ask me if I've ever been shot at. They are not joking. In some fundamental way, I just don't fit in, yet it looks like I am stuck here.

Of course, many of my students feel sort of the same way, which is why I bond especially to the kids who don't quite fit in the rigid social atmosphere here, the kids who, like me, think it's creepy that cheerleaders are assigned a football player and have to bake cookies for him and decorate his locker before every game.

And, as I said, my colleagues are driving me insane.

Some are incompetent. Besides the guy who requested the level-three classes so nobody would care if he wasn't working, there is a teacher who calls everyone "sweetheart," and nobody gets below a C in her class. (Her relentless friendliness also hides a passion for the status quo and a fear and loathing of anyone different. Caroline and I develop this personal litmus test where we figure that the few kids who see through this lady are really something special.) Captain Jack only periodically showed up drunk and then stopped drinking when he got cancer, so he's still there and sober and in remission, though he is still not really doing much teaching.

Some are racist. Last year, a teacher who should have packed it in years ago, a walking cloud of bitterness, was finally given the gate for saying to the one Hispanic kid in his class, after the kid wasn't paying attention when he asked a question, "Why don't you get welfare to buy you a hearing aid?" Caroline was actually instrumental in getting the kid to report this, and as a result she is a total pariah with most of the faculty now. She's also looking for another job. In my second year, the lady who runs the student community-service club has kids pretend to be dead on some drunken-driving-awareness day. As the day goes by, more and more kids "die" from drunk driving. They signify that they are dead by painting their faces black and not speaking. I complain about the incredibly racist symbolism, talk about Ralph Ellison and black invisibility, and she listens politely. Dead kids continue to wear blackface annually thereafter.

Many more are just old, tired, and bitter. They complain about everything. All the time. They don't show any passion for their work, and I wonder if they ever did. The school lets out at one forty-five. It's an absolute ghost town by two, though our contract requires us to stay until two-thirty. The people who are quickest to file a grievance when the administration doesn't adhere to the contract, including our union rep, are impossible to find by two.

Some young people have been hired, but by the end of this year everyone under forty who was there or was hired since I was will have left. Why not? Why stay here? These are not people who are in teaching because they love it—they are in teaching, by and large, because they wanted a dependable civil-service job, or they wanted to be able to spend their entire summer on the Cape, or they wanted to coach hockey. Teaching is an inconvenience.

And you can't ever talk about it. They are all so insecure that they view any talk about teaching as an attack. (Though from the little I know about the history of this place, sometimes it really *is* an attack, so maybe they're not as paranoid as I think.)

So the people I work with feel more like the people I work against. When I see the students for between forty-five and ninety minutes, and I try to get them to use their minds and open up, they are coming from hours of lackluster classes in which they are either beaten down, bored to death, or insulted with easy work.

And the worst part—and this is the part, I think, that is keeping me from sleeping—is that I am turning into one of them. On my worst days—days like tomorrow, for example, when I will be barely functional due to lack of sleep—I am doing a better job for these kids than most of the people I work with. So why try to be excellent, when even good enough is better than most? I am starting to mail it in. In another year, or two, or five, I will be mailing it in every day. And I will be bitter because I am stuck in a job I no longer love. I will be bitter because I hate myself and the people I work for and with. The burnouts' victory over me will be complete. I will have become them.

Over the course of several sleepless nights, I come to a conclusion. I have to stop working here. I would rather not teach than continue to teach here, because I will soon be the kind of teacher that gives teaching a bad name. This must be how people feel when they decide to end a problematic relationship (I was always on the receiving end, so I am only speculating here, analogy-wise). It breaks took off work to go have my interview with the human-resources lady. She was in Florida. Nobody had bothered to contact me. I went to the bagel store a few blocks away and huffed and puffed and clenched and unclenched my fists. Then some guy came in with a bunch of urban high school students and they sat two tables away talking about whatever field trip they had just been on with their cool teacher, and I just stared over at him, wondering how it happened that that guy has the job I want and I am still working thirty miles away. I went back a few days later and the human-resources lady emerged, covered in gold, hair bleached blond, nails as long as her fingers. She never apologized for standing me up. Her first words to me were "You can thank Brian Watkins for this interview."

"I have," I said, "and I will again."

She sort of smiled at me in a fuck-you way and started the interview.

"Let's imagine that you are teaching a class and a student refuses to do his work. What three things do you do?"

"Well, I mean, that depends on who the kid is and what the situation is. I mean, with some kids, you can—"

"No, but what *three things* would you do?"

"Well, which three is going to depend on the kid. I mean, I would probably try to talk to the kid alone, I mean, you know, you want to avoid having a big confrontation in front of an aud—"

"Okay, so talk to the student is number one. What two other things would you do?"

The interview continued in this way. It was completely pro forma, just to see that I wasn't a complete idiot or psychopath, or that I could at least disguise my idiocy or psychopathology for twenty minutes.

She told me that I would be put on a list of potential candidates, but somebody told me that the list was bullshit, and you had to apply to the principals individually. So I sent a résumé and cover letter, clearly indicating that I had been cleared for employment in

my heart, and I don't use that loosely, I mean it really makes
in the way that saying good-bye to someone you love makes
to think that I might not be teaching. But if teaching means
here, I can't do it. I'm still in love, but this relationship ju
working. Come January, I decide, I will send in my letter o
nation. This is well before the teaching job hunt gets under
I will be committed. I won't let myself get trapped by the s
the insurance, the pension, and I will not tell Northton Hi
we can still be friends, though I will say it's not you, it's me.

29

I AM SERIOUSLY afraid that I won't get a teaching job,
not in Boston. As I get older, I cost more to employ beca
union pay scales, which is great for me but makes it a tough
for someone to hire me because they're gambling more mone
teacher they don't know. Also, there is this weird urban/sub
divide in education. Suburban districts think urban teache
burned-out hacks who do little more than crowd control in
classrooms, and urban districts think suburban teachers are
pered wusses who have gotten so soft they could never hand
challenges of urban teaching.

All I want professionally is to teach in a small school in the
but every year I've spent in Northton has put me farther up th
scale and farther on the suburban side of the divide.

Last year I finally got an interview with the Boston P
Schools, and even got really close to getting hired, but I have no
if this is going to help me or hurt me. Caroline hooked me up w
Boston principal, Brian Watkins, who agreed to set me up with
interview at the main office in Court Street, something I had n
been able to accomplish on my own. You have to have a conta

the BPS by the fingernail queen at Court Street. I ended up getting a couple of phone calls and one interview.

The interview went strangely. The guy asked me about discipline, and I mentioned the fact that I'd worked in Newcastle, and that it was a pretty tough school, which is something many people don't know because rich people sometimes vacation in Newcastle, and then I gave my answer and he said, "Well, I see your tough school taught you nothing about classroom discipline."

What a dick! And I, for my part, was a disgusting sycophant. Instead of telling him to go fuck himself, I cravenly agreed that I had a lot to learn, and needed strong mentoring such as I had never had, blah blah blah. It was a really disgusting performance.

But I guess it worked, because at the end of the interview, he said how he really liked me and would call me in a couple of weeks. He didn't call, and I pestered him with daily messages until I finally got through to him, and he told me that he wasn't allowed to hire any white people, that the BPS was below its quota of minority staff again and sorry, because he thought I'd do a good job.

30

I ANNOUNCE MY decision to leave to the people I share my twenty-three-minute lunch with every day. For the last two years, this has included Terri, who, like Mr. Stevens, is still going strong after more than twenty years as a teacher and who, along with Caroline, is one of the only people here I can ever talk about teaching with. Whenever I feel ground down by the stupidity and evil of this institution, I look at Terri and feel some kind of hope. She is a mentor and a hero to me. (And, echoing the voice in my head, she always tells me I need to get out, that this isn't the place for me.) Mary Pat, who teaches next door to Terri and who I have really come to like, is my other lunch companion. I hated her my first year here—she was always saying the nastiest, most horrible things about kids and colleagues—but I have come to see that she is basically a really kind-hearted woman who puts on this front of being tart-tongued and frequently says whatever mean thing she can think of without fully checking it out for acceptability. I identify. Now she brings me stuff from her garden, trades recipes with me. This year she has Jeff the C-student football player, and, of course, Jeff's mom too, so we bond about that experience. Apparently Jeff's mom is telling her that her style just doesn't work for Jeff.

"Well," Mary Pat says to me, "you and I are about as far apart on the style spectrum as two people can get. So if your style didn't work for Jeff, and my style didn't work for Jeff, maybe it's Jeff and not us." Although we are sitting here complaining about a kid (well, really a parent), which is something that I thought was sick and evil four years ago, what I really like is that implicit in what Mary Pat says is the recognition that what I do is valid and that she respects me. This is really tremendous because most of the other old-guard teachers are horribly insecure and feel like maybe the teaching world has passed them by—nobody writes any articles in *English Journal* about how you should give lots of reading quizzes and lecture about symbolism for forty-five minutes—and their reaction is to belittle everything that's not what they do, because they feel like they're belittled all the time. When's the last time anybody told them they were doing a good job?

Terri and Mary Pat both agree that I should leave, but they caution me that I shouldn't resign until I have another job lined up. "But that's just how I'll get trapped," I say. But, they say, how can I take the chance? What if I don't land on my feet?

It's something I worry about too. I now have a kid and a mortgage, and I am asking a lot of my family here. Giving up my job security has the potential to really fuck things up at home. But then, so does living with a self-loathing burnout.

It's a terrifying leap into the unknown, but I know it's the right decision. Once I decide, really decide, that this is my last year at Northton High even if I have to go haul garbage bags full of fish stock again, I can sleep again.

So I scan the ads and plan to resign just before February vacation. In late December I'm looking at the ads in *The Boston Globe,* even though nothing is ever even advertised this early, and see an ad that says that Famous Athlete Youth Programs is looking for a teacher for its new truancy-prevention program for middle-schoolers.

I throw a résumé in, just for the hell of it. I get called for an interview.

Famous Athlete Youth Programs is located in a part of town I never go to and shares a building with a medical clinic. I arrive at the same time as a tall black woman, and we sit there in awkward silence for probably twenty minutes until I finally say, "So are they interviewing us together, or what? That's kind of weird."

"Yeah," she says, "I'm not into the whole group-interview thing." Then she says that she is actually interviewing for the aide position. They are, according to their ad, hiring a teacher, a "tracker" (van driver), a social worker, and an aide.

Some guy comes and takes the tall woman away for her interview, and I am interviewed by two women—one black and one white. I don't know who they are. The black one laughs at all my jokes, which is usually a good sign. They explain to me how these two guys at the Boston Public Schools got this grant for truancy prevention, and how they are excited to be "partnering" with Famous Athlete Youth Programs to create a pilot program; that the position is funded by this grant administered by the Boston Public Schools (Famous Athlete, whose name is on the door and who brags in interviews about his involvement with "his kids," is not actually funding this program at all); that I will be working for Famous Athlete Youth Programs and not the Boston Public Schools, so there will be no fabulous union pay scale and benefits; that the grant funding for this program goes through June, and that there is no, I mean zero, guarantee that anything will be happening as of July 1. I talk about how I am committed to urban education, that being a city dweller and a homeowner gives me a stake in things, and I basically try to sell them on the idea that I can do this job. (Later I will find out that I am the only applicant who is even remotely qualified, and that I should have let them sell themselves to me. Oh, well.)

I say the short guarantee is okay—while I'm not looking at this as a stepping stone (a lie), if nothing else, it will give me some urban experience that might get me noticed at an urban school in a way that my current, suburb-heavy résumé just doesn't.

A few days later I get a call that terrifies me. Edward, the education director at Famous Athlete Youth Programs, offers me the job. It pays six thousand dollars less than what I'm making now, there is no health insurance, and they need me to start so soon that I won't even be able to give Northton two weeks' notice.

I think about it for thirty seconds. I ask if they can raise the salary by a few thousand bucks to cover the cost of extending my insurance coverage through COBRA. He says okay. It still amounts to a pretty significant pay cut, but it is working in the city, ten minutes' drive from my house; I might never get this opportunity again.

I take it. I conduct this entire transaction on a phone in the Northton High librarian's office.

31

THAT NIGHT I toss and turn and do not sleep at all. First thing in the morning, I go to the secretary and tell her I need fifteen minutes with Joan, the principal, today. She pencils me in for third period.

This is a long time to wait. Finally I head into Joan's office and give the speech I have been rehearsing since about 2 A.M. I tell her how I'm really sorry, how I know I'm putting her in a terrible spot, but this opportunity to work in the city has come up, and I just don't think I can turn it down.

I cringe and wait for the abuse that I feel is my due at this point. It is January. The caliber of teachers available in January is not high. I have royally screwed this woman. More than that, I have royally screwed my students. After half a year of getting used to my idiosyncrasies, of figuring out how to succeed in my class, they are going to have to get used to someone else, and probably this will be somebody who's not very good.

Incredibly, the abuse never comes. Joan says she is sad but not really surprised, that she knew I wanted to work closer to home, that she knows that when an opportunity arises you have to jump on it, which is what she did when she wiggled out of a multiyear contract to come here, and she has enjoyed having me on the staff and wishes me luck.

Years later I will still marvel at this. Joan treats me kindly as a fellow human being rather than abusing me as somebody who is breaking a contract and putting her in a very difficult position.

Three days later I will be summoned to the office of the superintendent, and incredibly, though Joan is the one who really *should* abuse me, he will abuse me instead, telling me I'm unprofessional, that he's never heard of such a thing, that this move is going to cost me financially because the contract says I have to be paid at an hourly rate if I don't work the whole year (this means the paycheck I think I have coming in two weeks will never arrive because I owe it all to the Northton Public Schools), and he doesn't know what I think I'm doing, but he's pretty sure I'm not going to like this new job.

He calls up Edward, my new boss at Famous Athlete Youth Programs, and yells at him too, with the result that I have to stay an extra six days at Northton High. I am baffled by his hostility—is he angry because I am just the latest new hire to leave, because the fact that everybody who comes here leaves maybe says something about how fucked up this place is, or is it just a personal thing? Is he mad because somebody else has dared to steal one of his employees? I will never know. I have always thought of this guy as a wimpy, harmless phony and have never understood the venom my colleagues direct at him, but I think I've just gotten a glimpse of what he's really like. "Ohhhhhhhh," I think, "so *that's* why they hate him."

The next two weeks are, I hope, the closest I will ever come to attending my own funeral like Huck and Tom do in *The Adventures of Tom Sawyer.* I tell my writing-workshop class, the best writing-workshop class I've ever had, and I kind of start to choke up. Once the news is finally out of my mouth, one girl speaks. All she says is "Mr. Halpin . . . ," but her voice is full of sorrow and surprise, and I will still be able to hear it years later.

The kids are devastated, horrified that I have inverted the natural order of things by leaving school before them, and so they respond to the news that I have selfishly placed my own interests above theirs by showering me with love. On my last day I get visits from many of my former students—they stop by just to say thank you, just to say good-bye. One girl—one of the outsiders I have always bonded with, and someone with a lot of similarities to me in her biography—gives me a beautiful card with her artwork on one side and a really nice, heartfelt note on the other. "Is it out of line to ask for a hug?" she asks. I have always been very scrupulous about not touching my students, just to be careful, to not give the wrong impression, particularly as a young man with female students, but I'm leaving anyway, so I give her a hug, probably the first one I've given in four and a half years here. It's nice.

Another girl from my sophomore class comes by and cries and cries and cries, really she sobs uncontrollably, and I get the feeling that I am just one more in a list of adults she's cared about who have left her. And, I mean, you know, I'm not her parent or anything, I see the girl in a class of twenty-five for forty-five minutes a day, and yet my leaving is genuinely making her sob with grief. I feel like a shit.

The kids in my writing workshop, which was a semester class and so scheduled to end a week after I leave anyway, shower me with stuff, including a commemorative mug with a picture of me with them wrapped around one side and the words THANKS MR. HALPIN on the other. They make a binder with a note from each of them and their favorite piece they wrote in my class. It's awesome, it's heartbreaking, and it's wonderful.

So I am sad, but this is also really one of the best days I have ever had as a teacher. I feel so appreciated, and what is colossally unfair is that I am able to get all this love by leaving in the middle of the year and totally screwing my students over. Had I held out till the end of the year and then left quietly, which would have been the considerate thing for me to do, I might have gotten a few cards, but nothing like this. It is amazing.

My colleagues, too, give me gift certificates and stuff, which is especially touching given the fact that a couple of them really hate me and have nonetheless kicked in five or ten bucks—it's an example of the same kind of class that was at work when the staff gave a nice sendoff to a principal many of them hated. Later, when I work with people with no class at all, I come to appreciate this even more.

As I walk out the door of Northton High forever, Mary Pat calls after me, "There goes another one over the wall!"

Part Four

Famous

Athlete

Youth

Programs

UE TO MY old boss winning his pissing contest with my new boss, I am two days late to orientation at Famous Athlete Youth Programs. Initially I'm very upset about this, because I figure the team will have done all kinds of bonding. Surprisingly, though, I'm not at all nervous about the job itself. Money is going to be tight at home due to my pay cut, and this job is substantially different from anything I've ever done, but I find myself feeling strangely serene about the whole thing. I drive to work through three neighborhoods of Boston, and unlike when I drove past the ranch houses to Northton High, the landscape here feels familiar, and I feel at home.

It also doesn't hurt that it's much closer to home in a literal geographic sense. On my first day of orientation there is a terrible snowstorm, and, driving at about ten miles an hour the whole way, it takes me half an hour to get home. I stagger inside and begin to complain to Kirsten about the horrific, slow drive: "It took me half an hour to . . ." I stop midsentence and start to laugh—I never made it home from Northton in less than forty-five minutes.

The orientation turns out to be total bullshit, and the team doesn't seem to have done much meaningful bonding. The four of us who will be working with the kids meet each other. Sandra is the woman who was here when I interviewed, and she'll be my aide (I don't have the first idea what to do with an aide). Mariette is the social worker, and Devon is the "tracker." I really don't like the implications of giving somebody a game-hunting title, but anyway, what it means is that he will drive the van and go pick kids up, and if they don't show up, he'll go looking for them.

Our boss, Edward, the Famous Athlete Youth Programs education director, arranges for some guy to come in and give us a photo-copied sheet with pictures of bugs on it so we can write on each bug something that bugs us. It's supposed to be some kind of team-building thing. He has a guy who works at the alternative school for violent youth talk to us about security. He scares the shit out of me talking about metal detectors and pat-downs, and Edward says he is going to use some of the grant money to buy a handheld metal de-tector like they use at the airport when you set off the walk-through detectors. He never does. As it turns out, none of these activities will really have any relation at all to the work we do.

One day the two bigwigs from the Boston Public Schools who wrote the grant for this program come in with Tashina, who is a much smaller wig there. They have this air of authority—fair enough, the money is coming from them—but it is kind of uncom-fortable, racially speaking. These two guys are white and everybody else is black except for me. So they come in in their suits and pinky rings (!) acting sort of haughty, like they are dealing with their ser-vants, and even though they haven't actually said anything that's made me uncomfortable, it creeps me out.

They have the school administrator's gift for talking big about their expectations, and making it seem like this is a real and impor-tant program. Well, it is important—they had to spend their grant money for this year or they won't get their grant money for next year, when they hope to get a much larger grant to set up an actual alternative school for kids who are truant. Whether it's real or not will become clear later.

Tashina talks about how she and Devon will "go on sweeps" to pick up truants they might find hanging out on the streets of Boston in January. (Assuming they're going to find these kids on the streets in the dead of winter is a terrible underestimation of the kids' men-tal capacities, in my opinion. I mean, okay, they are truant from middle school, but they do have enough sense not to hang on the corner when it's twenty degrees out.) If said frozen truants attend one of our "partner" middle schools, they will bring them down here to the dingy basement occupied by Famous Athlete Youth Programs and get work from our partner schools so we can educate them. (I should be suspicious about the fact that there haven't been any representatives from our two partner middle schools at our meetings, but I am still all aglow with the excitement of this new career challenge. Moron.) For, um, a period of time. Until they are ready to go back to school. But no longer than three weeks. That should be enough time for us to "fix" whatever's wrong with them so they will be ready to return to the schools they couldn't stand to go to in the first place. Sure, why not?

They tell me not to develop any curriculum—that will come from our partner schools.

So we sit and wait. Orientation ends after three increasingly boring days and Tashina comes by the next morning to take Devon on a sweep. Sandra, Mariette, and I have donuts and read the paper. Edward disappears into his office.

Devon and Tashina do not find anyone hanging on the icy streets that day. Or the next day. Or the next.

33

INALLY, AFTER THREE days of doing nothing, except for Devon, who has been doing sweeps with Tashina, and Tashina herself, who has some other kinds of duties at the Boston Public Schools, we get a call from Devon in the van. He and Tashina have nabbed some kid on his way to the store or something, and he attends one of our partner schools, and they are bringing him in.

I'm excited. I'm terrified. What am I going to have him do? Well, whatever it is, it'll only be for a few days, because soon we'll have some work from his partner school. He is a chubby, curly-haired kid named Jorge, pronounced in an Anglicized way—"George." He comes in looking kind of scared.

He and Mariette, the social worker, disappear into her office for a while, then she comes out and says she's going to go do the home visit. This is part of the established protocol: the initial intake interview will be followed by a visit to the student's home, and then a report will be written.

Jorge is turned over to me. I am as nervous as I was when I taught my first class, because I have no map—and no idea what this is going to look like. We talk some about why he's here. Then I have him do a writing assignment and some silent reading with the young-adult books I've bought. Then it's pretty much time for him to go home.

I call over to the woman who's supposed to be the liaison at Jorge's school. She isn't there, and she does not return my call. She will not return my call the next day, or the next. I continue to improvise with Jorge. He says they were doing fractions in his class, and at this time the stock quotes are still printed in fractions, so I start a little stock-market game with him. I give him a thousand make-believe dollars and tell him to "spend" it all on stocks of his choice. We have to convert all the prices into fractions and divide up his thousand bucks, and then every day we check Jorge's stocks and graph how much "money" he currently has in his portfolio. We continue with the independent reading. I give him some writing assignments, and he revises them on the computer.

Every day Devon and Tashina go out on a sweep. Every day they come back empty-handed. I guess the word got out not to go to the store between eight and ten in the morning.

And yet Jorge comes every day. He comes early—sometimes he's there before the custodians even enter the building. He has missed something like fifty of the first ninety days of school, but now he is here with bells on every morning at eight. He tells us how he was in a self-contained special-ed class and hated it. I've been to three trainings telling me that self-contained special ed is now basically illegal in Massachusetts. Go figure.

Teaching only one student can be stressful because it's a lot more intense than I'm used to. Luckily Jorge and I get along really well—he is good at math (which is one up on me), and he genuinely seems to enjoy all the work I give him. I never get any work from his school. I do eventually get through on the phone, and the liaison tells me she will ask his teachers for three weeks' worth of work for him.

Having worked in big schools, I know this means that I'm never going to see any work at all. And I don't really blame the teachers—they have more than a hundred students each, and now somebody is asking them to put in an extra half hour at least to put together a bunch of work that probably won't ever get done for a kid who misses every other day of school. You can see why it's not a top priority. Eventually his English teacher sends over a couple of books with no assignments, but it's okay—it does give us some focus.

And then we start getting bad news.

The Boston Public Schools has instituted a pretty draconian attendance policy whereby you can't get promoted if you miss a certain number of days in a year. Jorge is way over the limit, and so we start asking the BPS through Tashina, whom we see every morning, whether Jorge's attendance here will help him get promoted.

No way, she tells us. Jorge is repeating the seventh grade no matter what.

But, but, but then we have nothing to offer him! Whether he stays here or goes home, he will be in the seventh grade next year. If he comes early here every day and then successfully transitions back to his school, which is our stated goal, he will be in the seventh grade next year. If he gets high and plays video games and never shows his face in here again, he will be in the seventh grade next year.

So he really has no incentive to come in here except for entertainment and "enrichment." Which is enough for now—hell, I've watched enough daytime TV to know that even looking at my short pasty self is an improvement over studying the nuances in your twelfth viewing of the Ab Blaster commercial. Still, I am amazed at the stupidity behind this—this program was created to try to get kids back into school, and now we're telling them that their year is a washout.

Tashina is infuriating as she parrots the party line about how Jorge has gotten himself into a situation, and our goal here is to get him back into school, and whether he gets promoted or not is not our decision or our concern.

Well, of course it's our concern—we all love this kid. I spend all day with him pretty much one-on-one (needless to say, there's not a whole lot for Sandra, my aide, to do here), and I'm not sick of him—that's saying something. He is fundamentally a really sweet, kindhearted kid, and those are incredibly rare traits in a fourteen-year-old boy.

Some days I give Devon a ride home, and he complains bitterly about the whole policy. "This is bullshit," he says. "I got into this to help kids, and if I feel like we're screwing them over, I am gone."

He stays, and so does Jorge. What the hell, he has the best adult-to-student ratio in the history of education, as all four of us have nothing to do but pay attention to him all day. (The sweeps still have not found any frostbitten truants huddled on corners.)

We debate whether to tell Jorge that he can't be promoted. Eventually we give him some sort of sugarcoated version of the truth. Tashina allows as how somebody—principal or superintendent or deputy superintendent—can grant waivers to the attendance policy and may be willing to do so, but there are no guarantees and it has never actually been done. We play up the slim hope in our conversations with him, but, as I said, Jorge seems to enjoy coming here, and we seem a lot more pissed off about the attendance thing than he is.

And then we get a call from Jorge's special-ed advocate. Because Jorge was in special ed, his grandmother got an outside advocate to help her negotiate the Byzantine world of special ed in Boston and make sure his individualized education plan was being followed. (Every special-ed student gets an IEP detailing the services and modifications they're entitled to, but making sure all the administrators and teachers actually follow the plan requires a certain amount of vigilance in any school system, and more so in a gigantic urban one.) Now the advocate wants to know if I am special-ed–certified.

I'm not.

Well, he says, then we are in violation of Jorge's ed plan, and this whole thing is illegal, and we'd better get his ass back into the self-contained special-ed class he hated so much he never went.

Apparently the possibility that some of the kids who skip school might be kids with ed plans never crossed the minds of the geniuses who set this program up. So that was stupid, but the advocate is stupid too. I feel like screaming at him, but I scream at my coworkers instead. "He wasn't *going*. How is it advocating for a kid to insist that he be placed back into a situation that he hates, a situation that wasn't working at all? He's here *early* every day!"

Stupid.

Eventually Tashina comes to tell Jorge that he has to go back to his middle school. He starts to cry. And then he starts to beg. "Please don't make me go back there," he says. "I hate it there. I like it *here*, I wanna stay *here*."

The sight of this kid with a tough façade crying and begging to be allowed to stay in this half-assed program in this stupid basement with an English teacher trying to teach him math and science with no materials or curriculum just crushes me.

"I'm sorry," Tashina says, but what she means—you can just hear it in her voice—is "I don't give a shit."

"I'm sorry," the rest of us say, and what we mean is "I'm so sorry to send you back there. This is one of the stupidest, most counter-productive things I've ever seen and I am sick to be part of it and I'm sorry, Jorge, please don't cry, I wish you could stay, I'm sorry."

34

A FEW DAYS after Jorge leaves, Tashina comes in and announces that they will be bringing us a new crop of kids from our partner schools, and that these kids came up in their "roundtables." I don't really understand what the roundtables are, except that a bunch of people, including Tashina's pinky-ring-wearing bosses, get together and talk about kids who are missing a lot of school. Or something.

Anyway, they bring us about ten of these kids, and they shock me. I am expecting the worst, a bunch of hard, really rowdy kids, and what I find is that they are just kids, really very similar to most of the other kids I've taught. I mean, sure, Ken is kind of scarily sullen, but what the hell, I've had kids like that before. Mostly they seem to me like normal kids with just one aspect of their lives gone nuts. In most cases they have parents who are absent or ill or for some reason just unable or unwilling to clamp down when little Johnny decides he'd rather play PlayStation games in his underwear on the couch all day than go to school, or little Tina decides she'd rather hang out on the corner getting high with boys eight years older than she is. You get the idea.

They are in the seventh and eighth grade, and they range in age from thirteen to fifteen. When they reach sixteen, they have no legal obligation to be in school, so they become somebody else's problem.

Tashina informs us that they will be bringing us work to do from our partner schools, no, really, they mean it this time. "You are not to do any new work with them," she says (this sentence comes out of her mouth with exactly that strange syntax, which is one of the things that annoy me about Tashina—she can't say, "They don't want you to start any projects with them," she has to assert her authority over me, which is dubious, since I don't work for the Boston Public Schools).

So, I'm not to start any new work with the kids, but there are ten of them sitting in front of me for three and a half hours, and what exactly am I supposed to do with them?

I call over to the schools, and, of course, never get my phone calls returned. So I improvise my own curriculum. Later Tashina will ask me for copies of my curriculum so she can show it to people from the partner schools at our roundtable. "You mean the curriculum you told me not to create?" I will answer. So it's that kind of operation.

I have English fairly well covered with the stacks of young-adult books I bought when Jorge first arrived, and Famous Athlete has provided us with some three-year-old computers on which to do word processing, so I am pretty well set for writing too.

Jorge seemed to like the stock-market game, so I do that as well and these kids like it too. All the boys use at least part of their imaginary money to buy stock in Playboy Enterprises, which they like. Unfortunately for them, though, not everybody buying stocks has the fourteen-year-old boy's appetite for a piece of a soft-porn empire, and the stock doesn't really move much. This is during the Internet boom, and they are agog when they see how much Yahoo stock is up over where it was a year ago. It takes us entire mornings sometimes to check the stocks and graph their earnings, because the fractions and the graphing are very hard for them. But they do it.

I feel like the kids are a little light on science, and I decide that if I were a science teacher, which I guess I am, the thing I'd really want them to know would be the scientific method, so I set up an experiment with a lab write-up in which they have to figure out which room in our wildly unevenly climate-controlled basement is the hottest. (It's still way too freezing for truants to be standing on street corners—not that anybody is looking anymore—but the rooms in this basement range from subtropical to inferno. The bathroom, as we will see shortly, is the hottest, which, coupled with the digestive emissions of the maintenance guys, who seem to live in there, gives it a real fire-and-brimstone kind of atmosphere.)

We don't have thermometers, or any kind of science equipment at all, but every day we get cartons of milk with the kids' lunches, and since nobody drinks them, I convince the kids to use half-pints of milk as measuring devices. I am proceeding from the assumption that milk will spoil faster in a hotter room than a cool one, which I think is probably pretty scientifically sound. We discuss why it's important for them to use milks with the same date, and why they can't mix the whole milk and the chocolate, which is the best we do in terms of calibrating the equipment.

The kids spend the morning running around the basement sniffing milk, and after about an hour and a half they bring a revolting-smelling, already-curdling milk out of the infernal men's room, thus concluding that it is, in fact, the hottest room in the basement.

They need some social studies too, and one of them actually has a textbook—one of these deadly-dull intro-to-civics-type volumes: *Our American System* or some such thing. I decide that they might better learn about Our American System by doing rather than reading, so I make the PlayStation-in-his-underwear kid president and divide the rest of the kids into a bicameral legislature. The House introduces a bill allowing students to quit school after the completion of the sixth grade, but the Senate, ever more measured, offers the eighth grade as a compromise, and this is how the bill goes to the president. The president, who is currently enrolled in the eighth grade, announces that any bill that requires students to go to school after the seventh grade is unacceptable and vetoes the measure. Representative Ken, who has been reprimanded on several previous days for his habit of calling everybody in the room "hump" (typically in the statement "Shut up, hump!" after the distinguished gentleman hears something he disagrees with), introduces a bill that reads, in its entirety, "I get to call everybody a hump." The Senate is unimpressed, and the measure dies in committee.

So this is the kind of stuff that I do. And let me say what is undoubtedly on some of your minds, which is that the fact that I am teaching kids in a large, prosperous city in the richest country on earth in this dingy basement with no equipment or textbooks or curriculum like some frontier one-room schoolhouse is a disgrace.

And yet I am really proud of these few weeks. This is the point when this place most resembles a real school. Yes, my curriculum is half-assed, and no, it's not like I spend endless hours trying to design a multidisciplinary curriculum in areas I have no expertise in, but the kids come in, and they learn how to do fractions, they understand the scientific method, they know how their government works. Now, I know this is a really dangerous trap—when you have no expectations at all, anything seems like a success—but fuck it. The fact is, on my own, I taught these kids something. Not enough, but something.

35

SO WHILE OUR first class is in attendance, here is what a typical day at Famous Athlete Youth Programs looks like. Devon and I arrive at eight. About half the time the building is locked up tight. Nobody from Famous Athlete Youth Programs has a key, so sometimes we'll all be standing there—me, Devon, Sandra, Edward, the director of education, and Clinton, the executive director, waiting on the stoop in the cold for a maintenance guy to come and open the building. Sometimes a student or two will join us—usually it's Alan, a super nice kid who does good work and seems to enjoy it.

Alan and I attack the stack of newspapers that Famous Athlete

Youth Programs gets for free, and typically discuss the Celtics, who are no good this year but who have an exciting new rookie. "Paul Pierce is Nasty!" Alan says appreciatively after checking the box score almost every day.

Devon calls the houses of all the kids who aren't there, then gets in the van and goes to get them. (This is how I know about John playing PlayStation in his underwear—Devon catches him at it more than once.)

Sometime about midmorning, Mariette rolls in. She later disappears, ostensibly to do the home visits, which are supposed to precede the kids getting services. She just barely gets to all ten kids in the four weeks we have them. The appropriate forms are filled out, but the kids never end up getting any services.

Eventually Devon and the kids return, and we have class from nine till about twelve, when Devon takes a couple of them over to a nearby elementary school to pick up the school lunch. They always give us too many. I end up eating a lot of Tater Tots.

After lunch we do a little more work, typically writing at the computers, and then we have "community meeting," at which Devon tries to get the kids to see the error of their ways by having a conversation or showing a movie or something. One day he brings in a really nice young man who talks to the kids about how low he sank in his drug addiction—how he used to laugh at the crackheads until he became one. The entire staff notes that Jomo, one of our favorite students, has tears in his eyes during this part. The crackhead is a nice guy—we talk about Jackie Chan at lunch. This kind of thing is the most the kids ever get in the way of counseling.

On Fridays we have field trips. Sometimes we try to make them educational—science museum, aquarium, et cetera—and sometimes Devon takes them to the movies. I get to see *Tarzan* for free this way.

This all goes along swimmingly until one day at lunch when Ken, Jomo, and Tina all head over to Tina's house, which is nearby and free of adults, and get baked out of their gourds. Well, at least Ken and Jomo are baked out of their gourds. They reek of weed, their eyes are bloodshot, and their eyelids look like they're made of lead. It's kind of cute, in a way—they seem to think we are either idiots or incredibly unobservant.

So they walk in totally baked, and Tashina just happens to be standing there, even though she's usually never around at lunchtime, because she and Mariette are going out to lunch. Sandra, Devon, Mariette, and I all just kind of look at each other trying to figure out what to do, and we can't ask Edward because he's out (he tends to take prolonged lunches), and so is Clinton, so Tashina takes over.

She gets Ken and Jomo in a room and starts yelling at them about how stupid and irresponsible they are, and how they have a lot of nerve coming in to her school high on drugs, and how they need to show her more respect, blah blah blah, and they are dismissed from the program. Go ahead and leave right now, she tells them, because you are gone.

Ken and Jomo stumble out, Tashina leaves, and the rest of us just stand there, slack-jawed. Okay, yes, they came to class high, but what are we proving by kicking them out? And what the hell did Tashina mean calling this her school? We don't work for her. So Devon and Sandra and I have this discussion, and Mariette stands there taking mental notes, because she is going to run back and tell Tashina everything we say.

I know this because Tashina comes in the next day and tries to smooth things over and says how she said "my school" the same way she refers to "my apartment" even though she doesn't own the building, it's just how she refers to places where she spends time. She disappears into Edward's office and has this long meeting with Edward and Clinton, which I guess develops into a pissing contest over who's in charge. Which is not clear. These kids are BPS students, we get lunch from the BPS, we are funded with BPS money, but Famous Athlete signs all my paychecks.

After the meeting, Tashina, apparently defeated, disappears and Edward comes in to tell us that Ken and Jomo are reinstated.

They come back, but the thrill is gone. All the energy has gone out of the class, and about a week later Tashina returns, triumphant, to announce that all the students here have had their allotted stay and must now go back to their schools, beginning tomorrow. It's after lunch, and we don't have time for any kind of ritual or farewell. They just leave. Of course, most of them will not go back to school.

Angry and depressed, I sit in the computer room with Devon and Sandra just shaking my head. When Tashina comes in, I tell her how it really concerns me that we're not helping these kids, that we're not really doing anything to help them, that they won't go to school after they leave us, they'll just hang on the streets, so what have we done here?

"I really don't understand," Tashina says. "You did your job. You have them here for a period of time, and you do what you're supposed to do. Why do you care what happens to them when they leave here?"

This is a serious question. Tashina, who works for the Boston Public Schools, doesn't understand why I care about what happens to my students. She really doesn't understand.

"If you don't understand that," I say, "we really have nothing to talk about."

She looks at me quizzically, gives up, and walks away.

36

ONCE OUR FIRST class is gone, most of the air goes out of our tires. We get a new crop of kids, but since I saw what happened with the first group, it's difficult for me to work up much enthusiasm for designing anything even as interesting and fun as the mock-legislature assignment or the stinky-milk lab. I come in every day and teach, but I have to admit I'm not doing my best work here. It's the same feeling I had only a few months ago at Northton High, the feeling that let me know it was time to get out. What, exactly, is the point of doing a good job? Nobody cares if anything good happens here. Maybe the kids care, but most of them do a great job of disguising it. Devon frequently has to go and pick up Maria, who lives across the street. Sometimes he will sit in the van outside her apartment and see her peeking out the windows and not coming.

Then again, sometimes she does show up. Who knows why? Only one student shows up regularly on her own with no need for Devon to "track" her. Her name is Kalia, and for the first few weeks I cannot understand what she's doing here. She is small and quiet, she works hard, and she seems to know a great deal. Why on earth hasn't she been going to school?

Well, one day it becomes clear when Peter, another of our students who is generally quiet, hits Kalia with a sort of randomly aimed squirt gun. (I know, I know—why does he have a squirt gun? Why is he shooting it in school, even if his school is this crummy basement? Very good questions. I have no answers.) Kalia's entire face tightens up. She walks up to Peter and says, "*Fuck* you, nigger." She doesn't yell it or anything, she says it in this really flat, really cold way that kind of scares me. Then she spits in his face. Though she is obviously flying off the handle, she doesn't appear to be flying off the handle, and that makes it scarier.

A few weeks later we have to pull her off of some kid in the park across the street who is twice her size and who, in my opinion, wouldn't have stood a chance if we hadn't intervened. Otherwise, though, Kalia is sweet, quiet, and really very innocent. One day she comes up to me and Sandra and asks us what an "O.G. party" is. We look at each other blankly as I picture something possibly involving Ice-T, which is horrifying enough, but then Kalia elaborates: "Peter was on the party line last night, and he heard Lourdes saying that all the boys should come over her house for an O.G. party."

We eventually discover that this means that Lourdes, on a 976-numbered teen chat line, invited every teenaged boy who happened to be on the line that night to come to her house for an orgy the next day. Peter says after Lourdes got off the chat line he heard some guys talking about "running a train" on her. So I spend the day having them write something autobiographical on the computers while everybody else makes phone calls to parents and police and tries to prevent Lourdes from being gang-raped this afternoon.

It's clear that these kids need a lot of help, but at least they are here and getting referrals to help, or getting some help, or something . . . right? Well, not really. Mariette has given up all pretense of working. She arrives between nine and ten and then disappears at noon for lunch with Tashina. Sometimes she comes back after a couple of hours, and sometimes she doesn't. I guess maybe the reports that need to get filed for these kids get filed, but it's clear that our full-time social worker is not really doing a hell of a lot of social work these days. Unless socializing with Tashina while they're both being paid to work counts.

There's not much happening in terms of parent contact. Except for Drew's mom, who seems to be in here every day flirting madly with Devon. We all tease him and get a laugh out of it. Eventually he drops some very strong hints that she should back off, and she immediately calls Edward and complains that Devon was sexually harassing her. "He told me I should drop the zero and get with a hero," she says. I know Devon well enough after just four months to know that he is just simply not the kind of guy to drop that cheesy of a line on anybody. We stop teasing Devon because it's unclear how nuts this woman is and how far she will push her false accusation. (It ends up being pretty far—dissatisfied with the response she gets from Edward, she tries calling the Boston Public Schools, but she is effectively stymied by voice mail and many layers of bureaucracy that I suspect may have been set up for the express purpose of stymieing any parent complaint and eventually gives up.)

So we can no longer tease Devon about that, but he did grow up in Indiana, so as a native Cincinnatian I can still tease him about that. Actually the nicest thing about working here these days is the relationship I've built with Devon and Sandra. The three of us make fun of Mariette for not working, and of Edward just because he's ridiculous (particularly one day after a prolonged lunchtime shopping expedition, he literally struts in wearing an African-print pillbox hat and looking completely stupid). We talk about how fucked up this program is and our worry about the kids. Many days after community meeting when the kids have said things that make us all cringe, Sandra and I will sit there as Devon drives them home and just shake our heads. "I really worry," she says. "What's going to happen to our children? How can I bring a child into this world?" (Sandra is engaged, and thinking about procreation.) I think much the same thing—I have a small child who shares a city with these kids as well as all the kids they hate and are afraid of. The world they describe is one of drugs, hopelessness, and endless violence paying back other violence. It's enough to make me want to move.

I have to keep reminding myself (and Sandra) that we are, by definition, dealing with the kids who are not making it, who are falling between the cracks. Indeed, for some of these kids, this half-assed program in this dingy basement is the last stop before falling through the cracks, and we do see a few off into the cracks: Mahogany comes twice, then disappears forever. Katie, who's pregnant, comes three times and talks about how she and her boyfriend sit in the house and watch Jerry Springer all the time. Then she disappears. But there are, I say, plenty of kids who are full of hope and ambition, kids who are fundamentally more like us than these kids. I'm not talking about race here, as Sandra is black and I'm white—but we share a certain belief in the value of education, in the importance of picking your battles and occasionally walking or even running away from a fight, a hope in the future, that many of our students just don't have. Despite the fact that I don't really work very hard here, it makes the work here very hard.

But if these values—along with a belief in the ability of the majority of these kids to turn it around and do something positive—divide us from the kids, they do bond us to each other. I wondered when I walked in here on the first day if being the only white person would be an issue. It turns out not to be. I mean, yes, I have to leave the conversation about corporal punishment of one's offspring, because there's just too great a cultural gap there, and when the issue of fraternities and sororities (of which Devon and Sandra are both members, brothers and sisters, alumni, or whatever people who belong to those organizations call each other when they're no longer in college) comes up, I know better than to even enter the discussion, but otherwise I find that it's not really much of an issue—I really feel more at home with Devon and Sandra than I did at Northton High, where everybody was white.

I definitely don't feel at home in this program, though. One of the reasons that Devon and Sandra and I get along so well is that we all hate the same stupid things about it. I like them, but it's pretty clear already that our work life together can't last.

37

S O THE AIR has been out of our tires for a few weeks when we officially become a joke. Clinton, the program's executive director, brings in a new student, Tania, and announces that she will be joining us for a few days while they wait for her paperwork to go through at her new school. She is a friend of somebody and was not referred through the Boston Public Schools so is not officially part of the population we are supposed to serve. But we have a seat and a friend of Clinton's needed a favor, so we are now in the baby-sitting business.

She does okay for a few days—she's been going to school more or less regularly and is slightly older than the other kids—and I don't mind having her in class even though she's not supposed to be here. She goes off to her new school, gets suspended or possibly expelled on the first day for fighting, and then is back in class. Only now we have another new student, Karima, and the combination is very, very bad. For instance, one day we are taking a field trip to the library for some kind of research thing I'm having them do, and as we cross the street I say something pretty innocuous to Karima, like could she please not yell at the top of her lungs at people in passing cars or something, and right there in the middle of the street she turns and yells in my face, "Shut the fuck up! You're not my fucking father, you don't get to tell me shit, so just shut the fuck up!" Ahhhh. Delightful.

Since we really have no rules or procedures, and indeed, since we are not a real program at all these days, I don't do anything about this. I just kind of take it (well, I am very very busy biting my tongue, because I have these verbal-combat instincts that it is my professional responsibility to keep in check when dealing with students, even ones who are telling me to shut the fuck up right in the middle of Dudley Square, so I don't end up saying that she is correct, I am not her father, because unlike her father, I have to see her every day, which is what I really want to say because I want very badly to hit back, but I don't, which is what passes for a professional victory these days).

So this is the way Karima is, and now Tania kind of gets that way too. They seem to have decided that torturing me in real time is much more fun than watching people torture each other on Jerry Springer. Sometimes it's not confrontational—like the day when they are screaming at the top of their lungs some Foxy Brown or Lil' Kim song about her pussy and the various things she expects her men to do to it—but more often it is. For the first time since I had Jimmy in Northton five years ago, I just can't stand one of my students. (I can still stand Tania, because without Karima she reverts immediately to her old self.)

One day I'm driving the van for our field trip to the beach in order to give Devon a break from driving, and I mess with the radio for a joke, and Karima and Tania respond with a torrent of verbal abuse that is very effective. I get very angry, pout, and refuse to drive. Once we get to the beach, I feel guilty and amazed that I allowed their admittedly venomous abuse to get to me. I buy a scallion pancake at a Chinese restaurant across the street and offer to share it as a peace gesture. Tania takes some, Karima doesn't. That about sums up my relationship with these two.

The beach is an amazing scene. It's a Friday in June, and although school is still in session, you'd never know it from looking at the beach. The entire population of the Boston Public Schools seems to be here—hanging out, laughing, throwing each other into the surf, and generally having a good time.

Sitting in a group of kids in one of the pavilions we find Jorge. I guess we knew Jorge wasn't really going to be going to school after he left us, but to see him here is really depressing. He tells us that he went back to school for about two weeks after he left us and hasn't returned since. He looks like he's gained at least twenty pounds.

Eventually we move on down the beach, and about an hour later we all pile back into the van and drive away. I look back and see Jorge, still sitting where we left him.

here and please tell Famous Athlete that his friend Mr. Dick Weed was here to see him. We all have a very nice moment where we give each other the universal "what the hell was that?" look, and then everybody just starts laughing.

This kind of thing just doesn't happen in real schools, or even real alternative programs. Sadly, it also proves to pretty much be our final highlight. As we lurch toward June, fewer kids come. Eventually we complain enough to Edward about Tania being difficult and disruptive, especially for someone who is here as a guest, that he complains to Clinton, who removes her from the program. This seems to take all of the fun out of it for Karima, so she stops coming. In a neglect of his tracking duty that I could just kiss him for, Devon never checks up on her, and it should go without saying that Mariette doesn't either. So Karima is allowed to disappear.

So we are left with Kalia who spit, Lourdes who didn't have an orgy, Maria who lives across the street and has to be picked up, Peter who got spit on, and Drew with the amorous mom. For the final day of the program, we want to have a big field trip, something really special. But nobody really cares enough to plan anything, so we ask the kids what they want to do. They want to go to the mall, so we all get in the van and got to the mall. Devon takes the boys and I take the girls, and we spend hours wandering around the mall and eventually eat lunch at the food court. As we're leaving, I turn to Kalia, Maria, and Lourdes and say, "Look, guys, I'm really sorry that it's your last day and we're doing this lame trip to the mall." I really do feel bad about the whole thing—it just seems to symbolize everything about this program: we had big ideas, and what we ended up with was this half-assed thing that didn't really help anybody.

But maybe the students didn't see it that way. "What are you talking about?" the students say. "This is great!"

On the way home, the van goes right near my house, so I say

38

THE TIME WHEN this class is supposed to leave—twe[nty]
one days—comes and goes. Tashina disappears into the bowel[s of]
the BPS administrative offices and never reappears to tell us in [per-]
son, but eventually the news filters back to us that this grou[p is]
never being sent back to their regular schools. So while with [the]
previous group the deadline was so important that the kids ha[d to]
be removed from the basement and unceremoniously dum[ped]
back into their schools with no notice at all, this time it seems [like]
nobody cares.

We keep getting reminded that our program is a joke. One [day]
we are sitting waiting for Devon to come with our lunch when [this]
ridiculous Mr. Showbiz guy kind of oozes in. He's wearing s[un-]
glasses (in the basement), a shiny suit, and a fedora (!). "Hello," [he]
says to us in an FM-deejay-smooth voice. "I am looking for Cl[in-]
ton." We tell him that Clinton's not here today, and he explai[ns,]
"Well, see, I'm a producer and manager, actually I've produc[ed]
records for the Blue Hill Boyz and several other well-kno[wn]
groups"—later I will confirm that it's not just me, nobody in [the]
room has ever heard of the Blue Hill Boyz—"and in fact I wrote [Fa-]
mous Athlete's theme song, he likes to play it when he's worki[ng]
out, it goes something like this, 'I'm a Famous Athlete believ[e it]
rrrrrr . . . yeah, I've got the feverrrrrrrr . . .' "

He goes on and on with this smooth, self-promotional patter, b[ut]
there's just something a little off about it—besides his crap[py]
singing. He is just so obviously a loser in an expensive suit w[ho]
thinks we think he's big pimpin'. After about five minutes, he han[ds]
us all business cards, asks if anybody sings. Tania says that she do[es]
and he says, "Well, let me hear you then!" She shoots him dow[n]
with, "Uh-unh. You're gonna have to *pay* to hear *me* sing."

He laughs in an insincere way and asks us to tell Clinton he w[as] good-bye to everyone and have Devon drop me on the street. I never set foot inside Famous Athlete Youth Programs again.

39

I HAVE BEEN applying for jobs for a few months now, having long since decided that I can't come back to Famous Athlete Youth Programs even if the grant is renewed, which it probably won't be. One day in May I told Sandra, "I'd rather be a sub than come back here," and I'm pretty sure I meant it, though it's pretty easy to say something like that and incredibly horrible to actually have to work as a sub. Or so I imagine. Let's just say that when you see them around the halls of schools, they never look too psyched.

By the time Devon drops me on the corner after the mall trip, I'm feeling pretty good about my job prospects. I landed both the Newcastle and Northton jobs a week before school started, so I know by now that you don't really panic about not having a teaching job until the last day of August. Also, I've had a few nibbles for the fall, and I've already landed a summer job at the same Upward Bound program that didn't hire me five summers ago, so I know I can keep the wolf from the door for at least another seven weeks. That's not very long, but I am uncharacteristically calm about the whole thing.

Upward Bound does not start out auspiciously. We go to an orientation meeting that includes "diversity training." This is a really useless couple of hours where we watch some famous documentary about horrible old stereotypical images of African-Americans (the fat, scarf-wearing mammy; the bug-eyed coward who says, "Feets, do yo duty!"; et cetera). It's okay as a history lesson, I guess, but it's stuff I already know and has no bearing on anything I'm about to do. It's basically "whitey is bad," which is pretty typical of diversity training in my experience. Weeks later when I have kids from Somalia, Haiti, and Colombia all in the same class, I will not look back on this day and feel like it helped to prepare me for the experience.

Luckily, the job itself is much better. I'm supposed to team-teach one class with another teacher, which makes me very nervous, but it quickly becomes clear that it's going to work out—Zach and I have almost identical temperaments and philosophies and even taste in music, and I am still, as much as I've tried to purge this remnant of my adolescence, a terrible snob who judges people by the music they listen to. The only big difference between Zach and me is that he's nicer than I am. Working with him here turns out to be a great experience, one I've never really had before in teaching. I'm used to working pretty much in isolation, and so it's very nice to work with someone who sees the same kids I see every day and thinks pretty much the same things about what we should be doing with them.

So that's fun, as is the fact that we're teaching the kind of kids who choose to go to school for six weeks in the summer, so the work is very easy. Also, we get a free lunch in the host college's cafeteria every day, which means unlimited fries—probably not a good thing for my waistline, but it does take a lot of the sting out of working in the summertime.

One day after class Zach and I get some actual diversity training. We are talking to some students, and one of our Haitian students reveals that she would never look an adult who was angry with her in the eye, because that is considered very disrespectful. Now, this is a pretty fundamental difference between Haitian and American culture in terms of dealing with authority (can't you just hear the angry teacher yelling "Look at me when I'm talking to you!" at a kid who's been trained her whole life not to do that?), a piece of information that could prove very useful in working with these kids, and the kids have to tell us themselves, while our "diversity training" consisted of trying to make us feel guilty about Aunt Jemima. Oh, well.

Classes are a real joy. I have one class of three students that I end up conducting in the campus coffee shop at least once a week, and this makes us all feel supercool and collegiate, and the kids really rise to the occasion. I have a group of seniors that I really like (and they like me because I get their references to *American Pie*, which has just come out).

One day Zach and I are walking out of work together and have the strangest experience. Two large, older teenaged boys approach us and say, "Hey, you guys know anything about people beating up faggots around here? 'Cause we're faggots and we hear that people have been messing with faggots here, and we ain't down with that. I mean, you know, we're faggots, but we ain't bitches, you know what I'm sayin'?"

I am so very confused. I don't know how to play this. Zach and I say that we don't know of any gay-bashing incidents, and the one guy says, "'Cause, you know, you guys don't have a problem with us being faggots, right? 'Cause then we'd have a problem with you."

So clearly the script here is (a) we say, yes, we do have a problem with you being faggots, and they kick our ass, or (b) (I think this is the one they are really hoping for) we say, no, we don't have a problem, in fact we are faggots ourselves, and they reveal—aha!—that they are not, in fact, faggots! They've only been masquerading as faggots so that they can find some faggots and kick their asses! And then they kick our ass. It's clear that they haven't planned for option (c), which is that there are actually two men walking together who are both heterosexual and not homophobic, so we say, no, we don't have a problem, I offer how many people from my church are gay and I have a good friend who's a lesbian if that counts, and Zach tells a very moving story about how one of his former students recently came out, and how he felt very honored that the kid would share that information with him, and that, you know, these guys should be happy and proud to be who they are.

They insist on walking us to the corner, and I'm pretty sure the wheels are turning in their heads trying to figure out exactly how they can move the conversation back to an avenue that leads to ass kicking, but they don't manage to and eventually send us on our way.

Once again I am glad to have been with Zach. I was fighting the instinct to tell them to cut it out, come on, what's this really about, but Zach's sincerity—which was unfeigned despite the fact that he also knew these guys were fucking with us—carried the day. Whew.

This is about as hazardous as working here gets, with the exception of one day when we are all at lunch (they feed us and then make us have this pointless daily meeting during lunchtime at which nothing of substance is ever discussed) and somehow the subject of Famous Athlete Youth Programs comes up. The remark comes from a teacher I barely know, but I am suspicious of her because I knew that she worked at one of the program's "partner" schools, and my interactions with them had not given me a very high opinion of either place, and also all the kids hate her. (I've found that the kids are never wrong about stuff like this. That is to say, they can sometimes be fooled, en masse, into liking somebody who's a fraud or no good at their job, but they are never wrong about who they hate.) Discarding social graces, and knowing that I worked at this place, she pronounces that it was a horrible disgrace that kids came from her school and did nothing with us and got promoted to high school anyway. Though I'm saying all kinds of really choice things in my brain about how they didn't seem to do too fucking much when they were in her school either, I try to steer the conversation back to relatively neutral, impersonal stuff about how the program was screwed up from the start and how it was a shame because these kids had all these needs that the program was just not set up to address, but for reasons that are unclear to me—I mean, this is literally our first conversation—she wants my head. So I offer, "Those kids got screwed," but she will not be pacified because this was obviously a personal insult to her, and she comes back with, "Those kids got over." I am angry for the rest of the day about the fact that my manners are too good for me to have told this woman off in front of a table full of people, and it is certainly news to me that anybody but Alan got promoted, but in the end I think, Well, good for them. I hope they did get over and get promoted, and I hope that some of them are seniors in high school this year and that they beat the odds. But I have to confess, I suspect that most of them came out of this a lot worse than the adults involved.

Let's go to the scoreboard.

As predicted, the grant wasn't renewed and Famous Athlete Youth Programs' foray into truancy prevention went gentle into that good night, though the program did get to keep the new van that was bought with the grant money. So chalk this up as a win for them. Temporarily at least. More on that later.

I parlayed this urban experience into a job teaching in a small school in the city, as we'll see shortly. Chalk this up as a win for me.

Sandra finished her certification, got hired by the fingernail queen on the spot to teach second grade in Boston, got the "excellent teacher" twenty-thousand-dollar signing bonus from the state, and continues to teach elementary school in the Boston Public Schools. A kid I knew had her as a teacher and said she was awesome. I'm sure it's true. All of that would have happened for her if she hadn't worked at Famous Athlete, but she managed to pick up some extra money during that critical end-of-grad-school period, mostly by watching me teach. Or, perhaps I should say, given the quality of my own performance, watching me "teach." So she was a winner here.

Devon got a job running a program for recovering substance abusers. He probably could have gotten that without the Famous

Athlete experience, though, and he spent six months working at this job with crappy pay and no benefits instead of another job that might have been better in either respect. And he worked harder than anybody else. And he had to deal with that bullshit with Drew's mom. So I guess this would have to go in the loss column for him.

Through the good offices of Tashina, Mariette got another job as a social worker. Count this experience as a win for her.

The recovering crackhead who came to speak to us fell off the wagon. We all saw him on the news being arrested for sexual assault. I suppose this is unrelated to his guest appearance in front of us, so let's put his contact with Famous Athlete Youth Programs as a question mark.

The pinky-ring–wearing guys were able to parlay their grant into a bigger grant for the following year, and did open a real alternative school for kids who are truant. They called me for an interview three days before school was going to open. I got petty satisfaction from never calling them back. Still, they got exactly what they wanted out of this experience, so it was definitely a win for them.

As for the kids, I have no idea. I know that Alan, the early spotter of Paul Pierce's talent, got his shit together, began attending school regularly, and got promoted to high school despite the supposedly ironclad draconian attendance policy. He came by, beaming, when he got his official notice that he would be in the ninth grade next year. I have no idea how he sidestepped the attendance policy. A definite win for him—for this kid, the program did everything it was supposed to do. We intervened at a time when he was screwing up and somehow helped him to stop screwing up and start doing as well as he was able to. So I guess that was a win for us too. As for the others, I saw Tina smoking blunts with older guys at the bus stop a few times and looking right through me, and then I never saw her again. I saw Lourdes downtown just a few weeks ago, but she didn't see me. She is seventeen and looks about twenty-five, and she was nicely dressed, as if she had a job, so maybe things worked out okay for her. I hope so. She was a nice kid. I haven't seen or heard of any of the other students since they left us. So I guess it's a question mark for most of them.

About six months after I left, Famous Athlete, who used to talk at length about his dedication to "his kids" in interviews, shut down Famous Athlete Youth Programs forever. I called an old sports columnist who always seemed to have a special hatred for Famous Athlete just to make sure Famous Athlete got some publicity for it. The columnist didn't disappoint—he gave the closure a few sentences in his column. It is probably about one one-thousandth of the column inches Famous Athlete got in the local papers for his dedication to the youth of Boston.

Famous Athlete has sucked horribly ever since he left Boston, but he built his legend well on the three good seasons he had here and the relative pittance he spent on a half-assed after-school program. Incredibly, many local sports columnists still talk about what a shame it is that Famous Athlete left and how much he did for the youth of this city. He's on his second team since leaving Boston, is no good at his job, and is a millionaire.

Part Five

Better

Than

You

40

OST OF MY early job leads for the fall don't amount to anything. Finally I get an interview at Better Than You, a charter school with a good reputation. I have been sending them résumés every year since they opened because the idea of the place always seemed incredibly appealing to me. It's a public school in Boston, but as a charter school, it operates completely independently from the Boston Public Schools through an agreement with the Massachusetts Department of Education. Charter schools, because they can be started by people with new or interesting ideas that might take a decade or more to really get going in a big school system, are supposed to be "laboratories of innovation" or "entrepreneurial education" and thus the salvation of education, or the future of education, or something. Reporters and columnists always talk and write about them in code, saying things like "They are free to innovate without the constraints that a standard public school faces." So liberals like me hear "They can do sensible stuff because they are not beholden to a ridiculous administrative bureaucracy," and conservatives hear "They can get those horrible, lazy teachers to actually work, because they don't have those satanic teachers' unions."

I confess to being a little nervous about the lack of a union (I always enjoyed my excellent benefits and automatic raises at my union jobs, not to mention the freedom to speak my mind and, yes, leave meetings at the exact minute they are supposed to end), but Better Than You was started by teachers and is run by teachers, and it's a chance to work in a small school in the city without having to deal with the fingernail queen or the BPS race quota.

So when my sixth annual application to Better Than You finally gets me an interview, I am very excited.

I arrive at the interview and am ushered into a room with about seven other people in it. They all wear these little pins that say BETTER THAN YOU. It strikes me as kind of creepy, in a Stepford Wives way—do they have to wear these, or do they all choose to because they're on the team? Such a display of team spirit is so foreign to my experience everywhere I've worked that it automatically makes me suspicious. And it's disconcerting to be interviewed by so many people. Who's the important one? Who's the one I should be most trying to impress, and who can I forget about? It's impossible to tell—I think automatically it's the oldest man in the room, but then this other guy is introduced as the principal. It's very confusing.

But the interview goes fairly well, and I start getting comfortable. In fact, I get so comfortable that I lose control of my mouth, and when somebody asks me what I do to relax, I say, "Drink heavily." Most of the people around the table laugh, and I immediately follow up with, "Whoa, I guess that wasn't the best kind of joke to make in a job interview," and a touching story about how hanging out with my two-year-old daughter is actually very relaxing because she totally lives in the moment. So things appear to be going well until this one lady, who's been kind of giving me the evil eye and not laughing at my jokes, says, "I see you left your last school in the middle of the year. Were you under contract?"

I stumble and say, yes, I mean, I had never actually signed a contract, but certainly the school had every expectation that I would stay through the year, but I saw this opportunity to make the jump to urban teaching, and I didn't know when that was going to happen again, so I felt like I had to take it.

"Well," she says, "what will you do if we offer you this job?"

"I'll take it."

"And how do we know that you won't leave this job in the middle of the year?"

"Uh . . . well, I guess you don't. But I wouldn't."

There may be more questions, but afterward I will remember

that this is how the interview ends, with me stuttering and red-faced while this woman grills me.

I walk out and find Zach waiting for an interview. We laugh and talk and wish each other luck. Qualifications-wise, he is just like me, but because he has more urban experience and is so much nicer than me, I'm sure he's going to get the job.

I go home replaying the interview in my mind again and again, especially the snotty gotcha questions about leaving in the middle of the year, and I stew and stew and convince myself that that exchange (plus Zach's superior experience and personality) is going to cost me the job. Fucking bitch! I mutter to myself. I've sent you motherfuckers a fucking résumé every fucking year, and never heard shit until I have some urban experience, and now you're going to hold that against me! Shit!

I go home and tell Kirsten how this one woman was an unbeliev-able bitch and I hate all those stupid Stepford Wives motherfuckers with their ridiculous little pins.

I send off more résumés. Two weeks later I'm delighted when the stupid Stepford Wives motherfuckers call and tell me they're checking my references. Three more weeks go by. I call the guy who called me (it was the old guy who I'd originally thought was the person to impress), and he doesn't get back to me, though I do have a nice conversation with his wife. I call the school and can never reach anybody, so I leave a couple of messages a week.

Finally, and with no explanation for the delay (during which I have convinced myself three times that I did get the job, no, actu-ally I didn't, yes, actually I did, no, there's no way, they would have called if I'd gotten it, et cetera), they call and offer me the job. I am happy and proud in that way that you always are when somebody offers you a job. I'm taken aback, though, when Chip, the principal, asks me what I would like to be paid. I've never negotiated for a salary before, because it's just not done in education—in a union school there is a pay scale, and they tell you immediately what you will make, and it's not open for discussion. Because I am so grateful to be hired, because I have always wanted to work at a school in the city, and because I made so very little at Famous Athlete Youth Programs, I name a figure that's on the low side. Chip immediately accepts my offer, which of course should be a clue that I have just given several thousand dollars away. Idiot!

Even still, my dream is finally coming true—I have a job at a small high school in the city, which is pretty much all I've ever wanted since I started doing this six years ago.

Years later I will find that my joke about drinking heavily was key to my being offered the job, and that the old guy put his foot down and insisted that they had to hire "that funny young man."

41

I'M HAPPY to have a job, but a little scared about this place. First there is the matter of the pins. It grows larger and larger in my mind and begins to feel creepier and creepier.

Then I get a call from Kathleen Shaughnessy, the English-department head and cofounder of the school—it's the harridan who was mean to me in the interview! Great! She tells me she's just down there at her house on the Cape with Roberta, who also teaches ninth-grade English, and they're working on the ninth-grade curriculum, and since I am also going to be using the ninth-grade curriculum, they thought they would call me! I can actually come down if I like, we can work on curriculum and then go for a bike ride to the beach!

I look at my calendar. It's still July. Are these people insane? Do I want to go be trapped in a house with two people I don't know at all and work on curriculum in July?

I plead family obligations—it is the first time in my tenure at Better Than You, but not the last, that I will invoke my daughter, Rowen, as an excuse to have a life. Summer is my time to be a full-time parent, (lying) I couldn't possibly get away, but maybe we can talk about this stuff over the phone! Or maybe I can just stick a fork in my eyeball!

So Kathleen and Roberta both get on the phone, and they ask me some stuff about ninth grade, and I am way too intimidated to participate in the conversation in any kind of meaningful way. I mean, I just got hired—am I going to say, "No, that's not the way I would do things, no, I think that's wrong"? Of course not. Well, a more confident person might. But I'm not that guy, so in hopes of ingratiating myself, I lamely agree to whatever they say.

But also, in the back of my mind, there is my experience everywhere else I've ever worked, where the curriculum is pretty fictional and nobody has time to supervise you. I have gotten pretty far by smiling and agreeing with people and then going off and doing what I want. Maybe it's just because I'm afraid of conflict. Whatever the case, they say some things I don't really agree with, and I just kind of smile and nod, or do whatever equivalent of that can be heard over the phone at your beach house where you're having a sleepover to work on curriculum, you freak.

So that's not good.

My friend Andrew knows some woman who used to work at Better Than You, so he gives me her number.

I call her up. "Hi, my name's Brendan Halpin, I'm a friend of Andrew's. Did he mention that I might be calling?"

I get a frosty "No. He didn't" and realize that my intro was way too vague and she is right now thinking about how exactly to kick Andrew's ass for giving her number out to a dateless loser, so I quickly explain the situation and try to work in in the first thirty seconds the fact that I have a wife and kid (so I'm not looking for a date, see), and I want to have a life, and I'm just wondering if working at Better Than You will allow me to do this.

She hems and haws and is polite enough to not want to say things that are too terrible, because, you know, I am going to be working there, but the impression I get is no, it's not going to be possible to have a life at Better Than You.

This impression is reinforced when I go in one day to talk to Roberta, who is back from the Cape and sitting alone in a classroom studying last year's scores on the Stanford 9, a standardized reading and math test that Better Than You students and all other high school students in Boston take every year. This meeting with her is something I agreed to in order to avoid having to go to the Cape. Anyway, Roberta starts out by talking about the way the school operates: teachers really have a voice in making policy; they create the schedule and vote on the budget and essentially get a voice in shaping every aspect of how the school runs. Hardly anybody in any profession has this much power in their workplace, and it's certainly unheard-of in schools, where teachers usually only have the power to complain bitterly about another terrible administrative decision. It really is an incredibly bold experiment, and I am starting to get really excited just thinking that I get to be a part of it.

But then Roberta starts going on and on about Stanford 9 scores, and I don't really care about Stanford 9 scores, and then she says something about how it's really great that Friday's faculty meetings sometimes go till seven or eight at night, and I just about fall over. She goes on to explain that the actual meetings only go until five (like that's any kind of relief. Five o'clock on Friday! Jesus!) and then everybody goes over to T. J. Dickweed's Family Fare and Pub to get loaded. "We work hard, and we play hard," she says.

She also talks about how everybody has a "Better Than You moment" when they freak out and feel like they can't possibly do it and break down. This she views as a positive and important rite of passage. She then goes on to talk about how great the place is in general.

Having worked in a lot of different situations already, I am suspicious of this kind of enthusiasm. There's always *something* wrong. But no, Roberta pretty much feels that this place is heaven on earth, and this conversation has done nothing to assuage my Stepford Wives fears.

What is up with the freaks who work here? I'll know soon, as I'm about to become one.

42

PART OF WHAT I've been hired to do here at Better Than You is to help set up a transition program for ninth-graders. It seems that many ninth-graders have been coming to Better Than You and failing everything in their first year and usually leaving the school during or after their second year.

I have never seen this fact mentioned in any of the fawning articles about Better Than You that appear regularly in both local and national publications. In fact, I learn, this year's senior class of twenty-two started as a freshman class of sixty-six. I guess mentioning this fact would ruin the story of how this school is reinventing urban education.

So if the local press has been asleep at the switch on this, at least, to their credit, the people inside Better Than You have not. They got grants to create this program to help kids who are coming in here with low skills to not fail everything their first year and to adjust to the demands of a college-prep school.

So far, so good. I mean, it is actually very encouraging, because every place I've ever worked has had problems, and this is really the first place where I've seen that a bunch of people actually got together and tried to do something to try to solve the problem rather than just complaining that these kids just don't get it. I remember very clearly a conversation I had with a history teacher at Northton

High: he was complaining about how terrible it is that the kids these days can't read like they used to, and it's that goddamn whole-language crap they teach them at the elementary schools, and then they do all this project crap over at the middle school, and now I have a class full of kids who can't read! In an uncharacteristic attack of boldness I said to him, "Okay, maybe it is the elementary school's fault—but these are the kids you have sitting in front of you. What are you going to do differently for them? Maybe they shouldn't come to you this way, but they do—so what are you going to do about it?" He looked at me like I was from space, because of course he was already doing all he was ever going to do about it, which was bitching about the elementary and middle schools.

So I am impressed that Better Than You has recognized a problem and decided to do something about it. I am even more impressed when I meet the people I'm supposed to work with: Jessie, the other English teacher, Alison and Sydney, the math teachers, and Lisa, the study-skills teacher. I like them immediately, and we all go out for Indian food on the first day of our meetings, and I just feel great about working here—I am in a room with four people I like, four people who obviously care about kids, four people who believe in working hard. This already pretty much matches the total number of people who really care about kids at any other school I've ever worked in, and I haven't even met most of the rest of the faculty yet.

Somewhat worrisome, though, is the fact that Lisa is the only person here who was on the committee that put the grant together last year. Everybody else who was on the committee left. Alison has agreed to be the lead teacher of this program, but she wasn't in on the planning. Sydney and Jessie, like me, are new to Better Than You.

So where did everybody go? What happened last year? Nobody will really say. Apparently the entire history department left to go start another school, and a bunch of other teachers just left. Lisa says something about how it was a difficult year, and that there were a lot of hard feelings when the old principal left (though getting rid of anybody who had faculty meetings till five on Fridays seems to me like it could only have been a good thing) and there may be some kind of racial element to these hard feelings, as the guy who left, or was forced out, was African-American, and the new principal is a thirty-year-old white guy with five years of teaching experience.

So this makes me nervous. As does all the work we have to do this week. We have to plan ninth-grade orientation and then run ninth-grade orientation and also figure out what exactly this program is going to look like, because a lot of the stuff that was in the original proposal has to be jettisoned.

This is stuff that Alison and Lisa leak out slowly over the first few days, but apparently there was significant opposition to the creation of a transition program from people who thought that it was groovy that so many students fell by the wayside because it proved that we had high standards. This group was, perhaps not surprisingly, led by Kathleen Shaughnessy. So when the original proposal became the final plan, all kinds of stuff got changed. We were originally supposed to have more time than the other ninth-grade English classes, but that got nixed. We were also supposed to have some freedom to create our own curriculum, but that too got nixed. So what emerges here is that we have to somehow bring some of these kids up several grade levels in one year, while doing exactly the same work in exactly the same amount of time as the other ninth-grade classes.

Now I'm feeling kind of leery about the fact that it looks like we've been set up to fail. We've been given an impossible mandate and no tools to accomplish it, so then when we fail, the people who were against it all along can say, "See? It doesn't work!"

This is pretty much the attitude of Kathleen Shaughnessy, who takes Jessie and me out for coffee one day, essentially to say that she doesn't believe in the program, and she thinks we'll basically end up telling some kids that they are in this for five years instead of four, and that this year will be a sort of tune-up for the ninth grade. Which is totally not what it's supposed to be. I just smile and nod, because this woman is incredibly intimidating. Everything she says comes from this rock-solid certainty that she is completely right, and it is very difficult to argue with that, especially if you only just kind of suspect that you are right. And, you know, she started the school and she's my boss. So I am trying not to piss her off.

After our coffee, Jessie and I go back to our planning meeting, and we all spend the afternoon talking about how Kathleen is this giant pain in the ass, and she wants the program to fail, and blah blah blah. I guess it's not very productive, but it feels good. Having a common enemy has really helped us all to start cohering as a unit.

And then a funny thing happens. I want a pin. I mean, I really want a pin. I see other people wearing their pins, and I want to wear one too. Only a week ago I was entertaining fantasies about refusing to wear the pin and seeing what would happen, but now—try and stop me! Kathleen and Roberta and their weirdness aside, I feel happy and lucky to be working with such great people, and when I put my pin on, I feel really proud of the place I work for the first time in my whole career.

43

NINTH-GRADE ORIENTATION and faculty orientation have been scheduled for almost the exact same times, which is a brilliant (and, unfortunately, all too characteristic) organizational move. So I am running a lot of the student-orientation activities (we are having the kids do things that will help us decide which ones will be in the transition program), then looking over the results of the writing samples after everybody is gone, and going to ridiculous faculty-orientation meetings in the meantime; school hasn't even started yet, and I'm already busting my ass for nine hours a day and coming home exhausted.

The faculty orientation, not surprisingly, is a horrifying waste of time. Most of it consists of people telling us how great the school is, and it's very short on practical information. So we get Kathleen Shaughnessy recounting, moist-eyed, the origin myth of Better Than You Charter High School: how she and our invisible co-founder, Rachael, worked together in an urban school, and how their classrooms had a connecting door, and how they used to see stupid things happen and horrible decisions being made, especially the case of Juan Diaz, who was simultaneously enrolled in both of their English classes, though one taught ninth-grade English and the other taught eleventh-grade English, and how they just knew that teachers knew what they were doing and could be trusted to run a school, and they worked for months putting together the application, and their dream is now a reality all around them. Or, at least, all around Kathleen. Rachael draws a salary from Better Than You working from her home 250 miles away in New York—nice work if you can get it, I guess.

When the time comes to decide which kids are going to be in the transition program, the transition department, along with Kathleen, Roberta, and a couple of other math teachers, stays at school until eight o'clock making the selections. I leave at four-thirty to pick up Rowen at her preschool, but I feel guilty about leaving these other people to pick up the slack for me.

This is something I have to get over, because throughout the year, I will usually be the first person out of the building when I leave at four-thirty. This is a sharp contrast to Northton, where I would usually be the last person to leave at three-thirty. So even though I now work about twenty-four miles closer to home than I used to, I'm not getting home any earlier. This is how you can tell we are educationally innovative.

Although I'm nervous about the ethic of overwork here at Better Than You, I still feel really deeply that I am home. Here I am doing what I've most wanted to do ever since I started teaching, and I'm doing it with people I like. At the end of our orientation week we are all invited to a barbecue at the house of one of the science teachers who lives in a suburb about a half hour from Boston. Now, I went to a couple of events attended by a large chunk of the faculty at Northton, and they always made me feel like impaling myself on an hors-d'oeuvre toothpick, but this feels different.

And it is. I drive out to Al the science teacher's house with Kirsten and Rowen, and we go hang out in the backyard. Al greets us warmly—at one point he takes me aside and tells me that the school is really lucky to have me and he is really excited to work with me, and this just makes me glow. Al has put together a really awesome spread of food, and I'm amazed to find that I'm having a great time. I get stuck talking to Kathleen for a few minutes, but even that isn't too painful. I just really like most of the people here. Rowen and I play games rolling down the hill, people are playing bocce, and the atmosphere is much nicer than most parties I've ever been to. And this is a *work* party. I mean, under the best of circumstances people usually go to these things out of a sense of obligation, but I am here having actual unfeigned fun.

At the end of the evening, as the sun is going down, Chip, our new principal, distributes little strips of paper to everybody on the staff who is there. (The principal is here socializing with the staff, and it doesn't appear to be too painful for either party! Amazing!) He has us all stand in a circle and take turns reading the little scraps. They turn out to be pieces of a couple of Langston Hughes poems and some other inspirational stuff. Yes, my alarm bells are ringing, this is corny, this is a joke, but I'm powerless against Chip's sincerity—my initial discomfort, as well as my precious skepticism and cynicism, turn to gooey sentimentality pretty quickly. After everybody has read their little scrap of paper, Chip gives a little speech about what great, important work we do, and how lucky we are to be able to do it.

I kind of stagger back to the car. It's just too much. The principal seems to respect the staff, and everybody seems to really understand that we're here to serve the kids. I can't imagine even the wildest apocalyptic scenario causing something like this to happen anywhere else I've ever worked.

I always imagined it could be like this. And now it is. I am really part of something special.

44

THE BUZZ I got from Al's party and from my initial meetings with the transition department never really goes away, even though the rest of the year manages to be really difficult.

Actually, the work with the kids is mostly just normally difficult. But despite the fact that I like and respect most of my colleagues, the work with the grown-ups kind of sucks.

For one thing, the cult of the meeting is in full effect here. The transition department meets once a week, and this, by and large, is pretty useful and necessary time, since we're planning and building a new program, talking about all the students, and reporting back to their parents about how they're doing.

The full faculty also meets once a week. These meetings are far less useful. Occasionally we make policy, but mostly we have departments presenting stuff to one another, or long philosophical discussions. They never really go till five, but they start at one-thirty on Friday afternoon and frequently go till three-thirty or four. Why do we need to meet weekly? I guess it's because other schools meet only monthly. Or maybe because, in the early years of the school, the entire staff (all five of them) met for hours every morning while the students did gym and Spanish, so to people who've been here that long, meeting only once a week feels like a terrible cutback, but it is mostly a waste of time made doubly annoying by the fact that it takes place on Friday afternoons.

I don't know how often this happens, but it seems like every Friday, a long-winded, superior science teacher ends up speechifying about some damn thing or another. The undertone of her speech is always that she hates white people, those of us in the room in particular, and we don't know what we're doing. (She, not surprisingly, chose not to attend Al's party.) It's unclear to me what she's doing here if she hates everybody so much. Sometimes something she says will enrage Kathleen, who also is long-winded and superior, and so many Friday afternoons we are left with Kathleen and Wilhelmina making dueling strident speeches, and while there is a kind of grim amusement in watching these two go after each other, mostly I just wish they would both shut the hell up so I can go home.

Because I am stressed out all the time. I have far fewer students than I ever had in Northton, and yet I seem to be working much harder. I always feel behind—like I have time to either correct papers or plan classes but not both. This is a terrible feeling. If my papers aren't corrected, I get stressed out because my kids need feedback, and it doesn't honor the hard work they put in if I just leave the papers lying around. On the other hand, if I haven't planned my classes, things don't go well, I feel like I don't know what I'm doing, and I kick myself for not putting my best effort into that class period. So I pretty much have one of these feelings going all the time.

And my English-department meetings don't help. Kathleen runs them, and they generally suck. Frequently there is some item up for discussion, but it's not really up for discussion. Kathleen pontificates for a while and responds to any disagreement with withering sarcasm. The best you can hope for if you open your mouth is that she will mock you and then come back with your idea next week as if it's her idea. The worst you can hope for is that she just mocks you.

I frequently do disagree with Kathleen, mostly for philosophical reasons that I won't get too deeply into except to say that when I visit her class once, there is some drill-and-kill vocabulary exercise followed by a "discussion" in which Kathleen asks opinion questions of the class in order to get them to say what she's thinking. It's this game of "can you read my mind," a lecture masquerading as a discussion, the kind of thing I always hated as a student.

So I am always uncomfortable in these meetings, biting my tongue to avoid verbal bullying. This is not helped by the fact that Roberta never disagrees with Kathleen. Or maybe she did once and they worked it out down on the Cape. In any case, she does more vocabulary with her ninth-grade classes than Jessie and I do, and she "covers" more books than Jessie and I do, and so we periodically have these check-ins that turn into "Why can't you two be more like Roberta?"

Ugh. Another English teacher tells me that things were different when the Old Guy was here because he was another big power center and was not afraid to tell Kathleen that she was full of it, but early in the year he disappeared for a week without notifying anybody or calling in, I mean he was literally a missing person, and then he showed up and wasn't given his job back, and this new woman was hired and ends up teaching not only the Old Guy's classes but also half of one of Kathleen's classes, which is kind of a neat trick.

We frequently have to go to Kathleen's house to correct writing exams or whatever, and this is actually kind of nice. She clearly likes to entertain, and she acts genuinely hospitable and pours us all giant goblets of wine when our work is done, and there is a real satisfaction in getting a lot of important work done with other people who give a shit. But there's this weird tension. On the one hand, it's nice and homey, but on the other hand it takes so long, and it would be so much easier to do at school. But for some reason we can't do that.

I also end up on a personnel committee with Kathleen. We don't do much except talk about all the great benefits, like family leave and life insurance, that regular schools have that we don't, and try to figure out what it would cost and why we can't have them. This is okay except for one day when I say that we are never going to attract more teachers of color unless we improve our salary and benefits. (For some reason teachers of color avoid this place like the plague— possibly because Kathleen is so powerful here and is given to saying things like, "Our students really have impoverished language and they need to listen to an articulate adult like me to find out how to express themselves verbally," which is a canard that's been discredited for years, and "*I Know Why the Caged Bird Sings* is an affirmative-action pick in our curriculum that really has no business there." I mean, okay, I'm not that crazy about that book either, because I think it's boring and sanctimonious, but God knows much of our White Guy curriculum is too, and Kathleen's choice of words seems calculated to be offensive.) Anyway, thinking of how Sandra was hired on the spot by the Boston Public Schools, I ask Kathleen why somebody like that would give up higher pay, better benefits, and greater job security to work here. Kathleen gets as angry as I've ever seen and says something incoherent whose key word is "fuck!"

So that's fun. In addition to all this stuff, I have to teach, and it's not long before I start having all these weird physiological symptoms. My asthma gets really bad, which it hasn't done in a long time. I frequently feel short of breath; just walking up the steps gets me winded. I go to the doctor and get some kind of steroid inhaler. Then I start having heart palpitations. One day I'm walking down the steps to the subway and I have to stop in my tracks, because my heart is suddenly hammering out of control. It scares the shit out of me—mostly because my own father fell over dead unexpectedly and inexplicably at age thirty-five. It stops after about ten seconds. More often, my heart will just feel weird—like there's a little hitch in the mechanism followed by one or two big beats that makes me stop and take a deep breath and wait for everything to get back to normal, which it does within about five seconds, but those five seconds really suck because I always think they are my last five seconds on earth.

I go to the doctor and get a King of Hearts monitor with two electrodes that I'm supposed to wear all the time. (It's about the size of a deck of cards! Get it?) When I feel something funny happening to my heart, I press a button and the thing records the event. I can then call it in to the techs at the hospital, who read the data. I end up annoying the techs for some reason—I call too frequently or not frequently enough—and eventually the doc tells me I'm just having normal palpitations, probably occasioned by stress.

Great.

45

ESPITE THE PALPITATIONS and the glut of meetings, I am deliriously happy at Better Than You. I say aloud in a faculty meeting early in the year that I hope to retire from this place, and I really mean it. For everything that's wrong with this place, it is the first place I have ever worked where everybody—even the people I don't like—really cares about what's happening here. Nobody here is teaching to support a house on the Cape or a golf habit. People are here because they want to work here.

Amazing.

But of course, it's not just the grown-ups that make it fun to work here—it's the kids. Not that they're much different from any of the other kids I've worked with. I mean, they are different from the kids at Famous Athlete Youth Programs in that the majority of them come from stable homes and don't need anybody to come and roust them off the couch to get to school, and they're different from the kids at Northton and Newcastle in that they are generally darker-complexioned and they talk much less about drinking and getting high. (I don't know if these kids actually drink and smoke less than their suburban counterparts, but they talk about it a hell of a lot less.) But basically, teenagers are teenagers.

My biggest thrill is that I get to be an advisor. What this means, well, nobody can exactly tell me. I am sort of a homeroom teacher. I give out report cards to the kids' parents when they come out. But I'm also sort of an unofficial counselor/advocate/mother hen. At least, this is the way I define the job. I just sort of make it up as I go along.

I don't have an auspicious start. We have a twenty-five-minute "advisory period" at the beginning of each day, and if nobody has ever really defined the job for me, they damn sure haven't told me what I'm supposed to do with fifteen half-awake teenagers during this time. I've always had a great time getting kids to open up using writing, so I decide that we are going to start the beginning of each day with a little bit of writing. A couple of game souls try it, but most of them just refuse. They're not hostile about it or anything—they just won't do it. So I quickly give that up.

Somebody asks me on the first or second day, "Are you going to leave too?" These kids are sophomores, and their advisor was part of last year's great faculty exodus. I tell them I don't have any plans to, that this is exactly the kind of place I have always wanted to teach, and I expect to be here until they carry me out. I have no idea if this scores points with them or not—most of them seem to adopt a "show me" attitude, which I guess is fair enough.

Many of my colleagues talk about the great conversations they have in advisory period about the issues of the day. I try to start some conversations, but I am hindered by the Great Schism: it seems that last year one of the girls in here talked to another one's boyfriend, or liked another one's boyfriend, or some damn thing, and now the girls in the advisory are split into two hostile camps over this issue. (This will, unbelievably, last for two full years.) So nobody wants to talk about anything while their hated enemies are in the room, which is pretty much always. (There are only four boys in the advisory. Mostly they play chess and talk trash to each other—"Awww, that's mate in two! You better give up now!")

One girl, Denise, refuses to speak to me or even acknowledge my existence. If I ask her a question, she will stare blankly. If I greet her, she will also stare blankly. One day I get right up in her face and end up following her out of her room to her locker making jokey banter the whole way. She stares blankly and refuses to acknowledge me. What did I do? I'm not sure.

So the advisory period itself is kind of a bust, although at least it gives these kids some time during this extended school day in which there are very few demands on them. As much as I feel like I'm working too hard, I at least have a free period every day—most of my students go from 8:25 to 3:30 with only a half hour for lunch (this is actually seven more minutes than the students and teachers at Northton got). If you have ever been to a conference or seminar or something where you sat in lectures and workshops for eight hours at a stretch, imagine doing that five days a week with two hours of homework to do when you got finished.

Outside the advisory period, though, is where my real work as an advisor takes place, and this ends up going very well. The way it typically works is that a teacher will come to me and say something like, "Hey, what's up with Will this week—he's had his head down in class." Or "I'm having a problem with Denise—she just seems to be giving me an attitude," or "Anna refused to take a test." Mostly they are little things, the kind of stuff that in a bigger school would go undetected, but here I will find Will at some point during the day and say, "Hey, what's going on in English? I hear you've had your head down all week." Many of my female advisees who can't stand each other hold similar feelings for certain of their teachers (actually for many of them it's the same one), so I am called upon to hear their side of the dispute. Mostly what I do is just listen to them and take them seriously. When we have a meeting with the teachers or whoever, I will usually try to present my advisees' concerns in a more diplomatic way than they likely would. I feel kind of wimpy and uncomfortable about the whole thing—I don't want to completely stick up for the teachers, because then I'll alienate the kids, but at the same time I don't want to completely stick up for the kids, because then I'll alienate the teachers. It's a weird balancing act, but I guess I do okay at it, because the kids end up talking to me and, usually, listening to me, and all my colleagues are still speaking to me too.

A lot of times when the students are talking to me alone, they'll tell me what an asshole a certain teacher is (more often than not, this is a person who bugs the hell out of me too), and what I usually end up saying—and this may not be the most liberating thing I could be telling them, but oh well—is that they are going to come across all kinds of assholes in their lives, and the unfortunate truth is that some of those assholes are going to have power over them, and so they need to start practicing sucking it back. I also do a lot of work on the fact that, no matter what the teacher says to you, if you tell him to shut the fuck up, you immediately make yourself the issue, and whatever he has or hasn't done stops being an issue.

I know that they listen to me, but I don't really see any immediate results from this lecture—indeed, one of my advisees racks up an astonishing fourteen suspensions. She also manages to have the highest GPA in the entire school for this year. Each one of her suspensions means at *least* an hour of meetings, as I have to talk to the student, the teacher, the vice principal, her parents, then everybody together. It's a lot of work, but it feels really important, and it's one of the things I am proudest of. I think about kids I have known at Northton especially, and how much they would have benefited from just knowing that there was at least one adult in the building who was looking out for them. I think it's one of the best things we do here, and so the fact that my advisees do homework or play chess during the twenty-five minutes in the morning when we are meeting starts seeming less important. I am also just really enjoying the chance to get to know these kids. When you have a hundred students broken into five classes of twenty, you get to know some of them, but a lot of them just go under the radar, and you rarely get the kind of contact with them that being an advisor provides. In some way I have proven myself to them, and we are then able to have good conversations (individually, of course) in advisory, and even the times when I am talking to them about how they just got kicked out of Spanish class again (these conversations always seem to come up right during the free period when I was going to get a bunch of correcting done) allow me to get to know these kids more than I've probably ever known any students. By the end of the year, seeing these kids is really the highlight of my day, and even Denise is speaking to me and occasionally smiling, which I happen to know from talking to her teachers is something really special.

I know I'm doing a good job about halfway through the year when one teacher who has had conflicts with at least three of my advisees (all of whom are female—are we sensing a trend here? No, unfortunately, we're not) and who believes that the student is wrong in any conflict with a teacher and pretty much refuses to examine what part in this he might have takes me aside and tries to tell me that I am doing my advisor job all wrong. "You know," he says, "the advisor is not supposed to be an advocate for the students. The advisor is supposed to help hold the kids accountable." "Holding kids accountable" is one of the great catchphrases of the school. Philosophically, it seems kind of icky to me. Couldn't we say something about supporting them or helping them take responsibility for their actions? No. We have to "hold them accountable."

My work with the personnel committee comes in handy here, because we have actually been reviewing the job description for advisor, which is in the massive draft edition of the faculty handbook that I was never given as a new hire and that the faculty has been waiting for, like, two years for the board to approve, and so I say, "Actually, the advisor is supposed to be an advocate. That very word is in the job description."

At the end of the year this teacher asks if we can have lunch so we can talk about how I don't have a problem with all these kids that he has a problem with. I don't know what to say—I mean, I try to take them seriously and treat them with respect, so that's not exactly a secret, but I also have a special advantage in that I see them every day but don't give them grades or homework. The fact that this guy even approached me about this makes me feel good—both for the ego strokes of feeling like I am doing something right (I've come far enough in this business that other people are asking *me* for advice!) and because it shows that, as much as this guy torments my advisees and appears to have a terrible rapport with them, he is at least open-minded enough to think about doing something different.

46

IN ADDITION TO my advisory, I am teaching two English classes. Each one meets for eighty minutes a day. These end up going pretty well despite the facts that I have no time to plan or correct and that in one of them I am supposed to be bringing kids up by four-plus grade levels in the same time the other kids have, while force-feeding them *The Odyssey* and *Julius Caesar,* along with other easy-to-read classics.

Having Jessie here helps immensely. We both have our desks in this enormous room in the basement (along with two other teachers) that is also our classroom, so it's really easy to just turn around and say, "Hey, I'm thinking about doing this with my class tomorrow—what do you think?" It's also very nice to have somebody here to commiserate with after department meetings. "She's tweaked" is Jessie's usual response to whatever heinous thing Kathleen has said this week.

What also happens because of the unusual desk arrangement is that we get to see each other's classes all the time. Space is at a premium for everyone in Boston, and perhaps especially for a non-profit school with no money, so basically there is no place to work other than in this room, so I am always in here working when Jessie is teaching, and she is frequently in here when I'm teaching.

This arrangement turns out to be one of the greatest things to happen to me as a teacher, and it's accidental. It's funny, because the department is trying to get us to visit other English teachers, and I do a couple of times (and of course I get supervisory visits from Kathleen, who is shockingly kind about what's happening, which is incomprehensible. She is cutting about our philosophical differences in meetings, but when she comes into my class, she is very gracious and gives me good feedback), but that is just too big a pain in the ass and stops happening after the first month or so. But I am in Jessie's class almost every day, and I end up seeing a great deal of the history classes that take place in here too. And what's really great about being in a class frequently, not just as a visitor, is that I get a lot more confident about my abilities. I see days when the kids are amazing, and I see days when the teachers are really struggling and the kids are out of control. So, you know, it's not just me. This is just so liberating, because I have spent most of my career behind my little door feeling like everybody but me knew exactly what they were doing, and nobody was struggling like I was. Now I see that everybody is. It reminds me of nothing so much as being a teenager—you sit in your room feeling like you are hideous because you have zits or whatever, and you think about how uncool you are really and how everybody else is so cool and if they only knew the real you, they would hate you. And then you start comparing notes when you get older and realize that every single person was having the same thoughts behind the closed door of their bedroom. So teaching adolescents turns out to be remarkably like being an adolescent. Which is a scary thought that probably has psychological implications I don't think I want to get into.

My "regular" freshman class goes very well almost from the beginning. I have a couple of girls who like to talk to each other a lot more than they like doing anything else, but that is pretty standard in a ninth-grade class. By and large, these kids have been successful in school, and they do the work and do it well, and enough of them do their reading assignments that we are able to have some really good discussions.

My "transition" class is more of a struggle almost immediately. For one thing, I have two kids in here who have pretty severe special needs. What I mean is that they are cognitively impaired in such a way that they are nowhere near where they need to be in the ninth grade, and they are going to need some serious one-on-one intervention to get there.

I'm tying myself in knots not to say anything about these kids that could ever be interpreted as unkind, but not surprisingly, the other kids are not quite so delicate. They see these kids and immediately feel, like the kids I had so long ago in Newcastle, that this is "the retard class." So they start going out of their way to separate themselves from the other kids by being mean to them. We just about get beyond that when both of these kids are "counseled out" of the school, which is a fancy way of saying that the special-ed director sits down with the parents and tells them that we can't serve their kids here, which I think is kind of dicey from a legal standpoint, but in any case, we are able to recommend some programs in the regular public schools that are more suitable for them. So we exist not as a counterexample to the regular public schools but as a sort of parasitic organism. Because there is somewhere for us to send these kids, we don't have to spend all kinds of money creating programs for them, which would divert money from our small class sizes and lower our test scores.

I sit in on one of these meetings with Cicely, an incredibly sweet girl with pretty severe special needs who all the teachers love. I am horrified as the special-ed director tells Cicely's mom how pretty Cicely is, how sweet Cicely is, how much we all love Cicely, and how Cicely really needs to go somewhere else. Tears spill out of Cicely's eyes during the whole speech, and finally she says, "I don't *want* to go to another school! I really like it here!" and it's like I have been time-warped back to the meeting with Jorge at Famous Athlete, and once again I have the sick feeling that a kid I really care about is getting screwed.

At some point after Cicely's departure, we end up having what will become known as "the transition talk," in which the class sounds off about everything that's bugging them. Tallulah is angry about Cicely being kicked out. I try to explain that she wasn't kicked out. Harrison complains about having a different schedule. Barry hates this corny school. I offer lamely that, like, 40 percent of the freshman class used to fail at this school, and that they (and this is the really uncomfortable part), not because they are dumb, because the whole program is really predicated on the idea that they are not dumb but just need some more work, have been identified as the kids who were at high risk for failing everything, and this is really trying to help them, blah blah blah. It's all true, but nobody wants to hear that somebody thinks they might fail, and nobody can believe it when I say we think you would have failed but we don't think you're dumb. It's true, but it's so foreign to anything they've ever heard before that they think I'm full of shit.

Despite this, though, I manage to forge a pretty good relationship with them. They make up a nickname for me, which is almost always a good sign. Well, they don't actually make it up, but they adopt it and make it their own. They call me "Mr. Chips." Some kid who's not my student gives me this name because I'm "mad corny," and he doesn't even know that Mr. Chips is some kind of hero teacher from the movies, it's just a play on corn chips, but my transition class starts calling me first Mr. Chips, then later just "Chips," which is when I know for sure it's affectionate. "Aw, come on, Chips," Travis will say when I give homework. In fact, while this nickname will never catch on with any of my other students (my advisees will end up calling me "Big H," which I suppose starts out ironically because, you know, I'm really not that big), this particular group of kids will continue to use it with me for the next two years. And I will like it way more than I could ever let on.

Early in the year, Jessie has this idea that we should put on a mock trial for George for our final project on *Of Mice and Men*. With the help of everybody else in the transition department, we end up doing this sometime in November. It's a huge hit. We do it at night with parents present, and it's my class for the prosecution and Jessie's for the defense. The lawyers dress up in suits, the migrant farmworkers dress up in overalls, Curley's wife dresses like a . . . well, appropriately, and Chip, the principal, serves as the judge. It is a spectacular success—the kids construct arguments very well, they speak well in front of a crowd that for most of them includes their parents, and they succeed at school, which is something that many of them tell us they have never done.

It measurably improves the tone of the class for weeks. But before long it goes downhill again—we have a student in this class who walks with crutches, and the kids start picking on him because he gets all kinds of special treatment. At first I can't believe how these kids are being cruel to a cripple, but eventually it becomes clear that the kid is just really hard to get along with. He stirs something up quietly, then watches as the other person flies off the handle and gets in trouble. Or sometimes he flies off the handle but doesn't get in trouble. This is because his mom is a gigantic pain in the ass who comes in with the "what the hell is wrong with you for wrongfully accusing my baby" routine every time he gets in trouble, so our vice principal, who is big into "holding kids accountable," stops holding him accountable, and the kids notice that the kid with the crutches gets away with all kinds of shit that they would get in trouble for, and it is a mess that never really gets solved.

I find out that I have totally misinterpreted the situation when I yell at the class after this kid, Vladimir (he's not Russian—go figure), leaves the room because somebody says something, and I totally blow my stack and say, "Look! In this life you are going to have to work with people you don't like! You don't have to like everybody, but you have to shut up about it!"

At this, Josette, who is pretty much the star student of this class both behaviorally and academically, the kid who is our poster child for the success of this transition program, because she always sat in the back of the room feeling stupid in previous grades and now she is doing really well, in fact she will be the only student I will ever give a 100 to on a piece of writing because it is just that freakin' good, lets me have it. She gets furious and starts yelling: "Don't you tell me to shut up! That kid annoys me every day when I am trying to learn and nothing ever happens to him, and if I say anything, you tell me to shut up! Well, I won't shut up!" Eventually she calms down and I apologize and realize that my whole take on this thing was wrong wrong wrong. Ooops.

Vlad and Barry, another student who is otherwise calm and cooperative, seem to have a special antagonism, and Barry starts obsessing about Vlad's behavior, so that even when Vlad is not specifically bugging him, Barry is getting angry about whatever it is that Vlad is doing, and this usually ends up with them both yelling at each other to fuck off, nigger, and this gets them automatic trips to the office of Erik, the vice principal, and Barry gets sent home for the day and Vlad doesn't.

After about the third or fourth time this happens, I am wondering aloud in the teachers' room what can be done about this situation, and Kathleen says, "Go down and take Barry out for a cup of coffee or a soda or something and just tell him that he's not crazy. Tell him that Vlad *is* getting special treatment, and you know it's not fair, but he has to focus on himself."

So I take Barry down for a soda or something, and I tell him that he's not crazy, and that what's happening is unfair and totally sucks, and I'm sorry. "It's mad *frustrating*," Barry says, and I say, yeah, I guess it probably is, and he says, "Something about that kid just gets me mad heated," and I say, yeah, you're not the only one (I don't tell him that at least three other teachers have expressed similar feelings). It doesn't solve the problem, but it's a nice human connection with a kid, and I appreciate the fact that Kathleen gave me both the advice and the permission to do this.

By the end of the year, things calm down somewhat because everyone can see the light at the end of the tunnel. Barry and almost everyone else in the class stays, and Vlad's mom withdraws him from school in a hail of recriminations, complaints to the Department of Education, and threats to sue.

(Four years later, Vladimir's mom almost runs my daughter down with a stroller in the mall and doesn't acknowledge that either my daughter or I are there. Vlad is with her, though, and he gives me a friendly hello. I stop and have a brief conversation with him and find him very pleasant and articulate. His mom is obviously exactly the same, but he, at least, seems transformed.)

When spring comes, we have suffered through *The Odyssey*, we have suffered through *I Know Why the Caged Bird Sings* (though we haven't suffered as much as we did with *The Odyssey*, no matter what Kathleen says), and the next item on the curriculum is *Julius*

Caesar. Well, *Julius Caesar,* in case you've never read it, totally sucks, and is way less accessible to teenagers than *Romeo and Juliet,* so Jessie and I bring this up in the department meeting, and Kathleen says she once had a student who killed him- or herself, so the play that ends with the teen suicides is not happening, and the discussion is pretty much over.

So, in the tradition of teachers everywhere, we decide to do *Romeo and Juliet* anyway. It works great. Jessie makes these fake swords with dowels and silver spray paint and we both have a great time putting scenes together with our classes. One day Erik, the vice principal, strolls by when we are rehearsing and completely spontaneously gives an hour of his time to train the kids in stage combat, which is something I had no idea he knew about and would never have known to ask him. I end up taking my classes over to a nearby park with a little amphitheater to practice their scenes, and this is great because it's a nice day and we're outside (and, unlike when I tried this at Northton, there is nobody to complain about the noise except a few people hitting balls on the nearby tennis courts), and though I freak out when Shane, as Romeo, and Malika, as Tybalt, get a little carried away in their sword fight and whack their "swords" together so hard that one shatters and a really nasty, splintery end comes flying at my head, overall it's a really positive experience. When we have to actually perform the scenes we get several days of rain, so we end up doing them inside, but it's still fun, and more important, the kids do not leave at the end of it feeling like Shakespeare totally sucks, which should really be the greatest goal of a kid's introduction to Shakespeare if you ask me, but nobody was asking me, because they worked really hard on this curriculum last year and, lest we forget, fine-tuned it on the Cape. Whatever. It is an irony that Jessie and I remark upon that this is supposed to be a "teacher-driven" school, whatever that means (it seems to mean that teachers do a lot of administrative work, though we do also get to approve the budget, which is a really unheard-of power), but here we are, teachers trying to drive, and we are told we can't do it. We suspect that maybe Kathleen had a particular teacher in mind when she founded a school based on teacher leadership.

Anyway, Kathleen throws a fit, and I always suspect that Roberta does too, and so Jessie and I get called on the carpet and have to go have this meeting with Chip, the principal, and Kathleen. She says all kinds of stuff about how *Julius Caesar* is critical to the curriculum because all the main works ask this question about who gets to lead, and this is critical to the school's civic mission. Which I happen to know is complete bullshit anyway. Once a week we have a "town meeting" in which kids are supposed to debate the issues of the day, but of course what they really want to debate is school policy, but they are not really allowed to, or when they do, their decisions carry no weight in terms of policy making, so in the name of teaching them about democracy, we are in fact teaching them that their voices and concerns don't matter, which they probably could have figured out just by looking at how many city services they don't get in their neighborhoods and didn't need a special school for.

Anyway, *Julius Caesar* is somehow critical to this. Jessie and I are pretty unrepentant, and the issue is not really resolved, but we at least all get to say our piece. Chip has another meeting to get to, and as the meeting winds down and we've been back and forth about seven times, I find some weird reserve of courage and say to Kathleen, "I feel like our department meetings are always about 'why can't you be more like Roberta.' We never brought this up for discussion at a department meeting because we can't discuss anything in department meetings; we can only argue, and you're much better at that than I am." She doesn't respond, and except for a smile at my nod to her debating skills, I have no idea what she thinks about what I just said. It feels good to get this stuff off my chest, but it doesn't really solve the debate that was at the heart of the matter.

47

THE SCHOOL YEAR kind of grinds to an end. The last big thing that happens is that the faculty votes to change the schedule for next year. Andres, a Spanish teacher, has created this schedule, and Sydney perfected it, so it's totally a homegrown phenomenon. Although the debate itself is kind of tiresome, the fact that we're having it is exciting. We are changing the schedule to something we think will be better for us not because some consultant rammed the idea down our throats but because one of our own thought it up and convinced us all, and we get to make the decision. This probably sounds incredibly mundane, but it's a degree of power over my work life that I have never had before, and it's thrilling.

We do a great job creating and changing a schedule, but we seem not to be doing such a hot job of retaining our staff. Jessie is pregnant and not returning. Two of the three new history teachers are not returning. Neither are the woman who replaced the Old Guy in the English department, the director of special education, a math teacher, the long-winded, whitey-hating science teacher, and the guidance counselor. It's not entirely clear what the problem is, but it's clear that there is a problem. Yet nobody seems to want to talk about it. Perhaps most surprisingly, Kathleen Shaughnessy is also leaving. She is going off to teach in some foreign country or something. At the time I figure it's probably because she's kind of a control freak, and the school has now grown so much that she can't really control it anymore, and so rather than be a bit player she's going to leave.

She makes noises to that effect—time for the school to grow, she will only get in the way, blah blah. It won't be until much later that I will figure out that she saw the shit en route to the fan much earlier than the rest of us did, so she bailed before she could get splattered.

I don't even think of leaving. In fact, I get a call from an old ed-school classmate telling me the school where she works is hiring.

They have, like, no men in their English department, she says, and they're willing to spend money to hire an experienced teacher. They can't find any candidates, she says. She is about 75 percent sure that if I interview, I'll get the job, she says. She works in an established high school with a union and a decent pay scale and benefits, and in all the material ways, it would probably be a better job, but my heart is really here, despite all the flaws.

Sometimes I see my students on the subway, or when I'm walking around my neighborhood in Boston, and it feels good. It gives me this kind of *It's a Wonderful Life,* small-town buzz in the middle of the big city. There goes Mr. Halpin! He's the schoolteacher!

So I don't even interview for the other job. And I feel pretty good about this, especially knowing that Kathleen isn't going to return. At the end of the year after classes are over we have a curriculum meeting that totally sucks. I say, hey, I'd like to teach *Romeo and Juliet* next year, and Roberta says no, it's really important that we give it two years with *Julius Caesar,* and I just about lose my mind. Now this is partly due to the fact that I am selling my condo and trying to buy another house, and there are all kinds of complications and snags, mostly brought on by the fact that my downstairs neighbor in the place I'm selling is a complete asshole, but it's also due to the fact that I have had a long, stressful year, it's supposed to be summer, and I'm sitting in this fucking meeting to talk about how we can't change the curriculum.

So I yell something along the lines of, "Listen, if we can't change anything, then what the hell am I doing here? Why am I spending a beautiful summer day sitting in a meeting about how we have to keep the curriculum exactly the same! I have to go!" So I storm out. This is the first time I have ever stormed out of a meeting. Later I come back contrite, but I have pretty well killed whatever momentum a meeting about how nothing can change could possibly have, so it fizzles out.

A couple of days later we have an end-of-the-year dinner at Kathleen's house. It's perfectly pleasant—she is really a top-notch entertainer—and, as I'm leaving, she says, "Well, Mr. Halpin, we had our moments, but remember—we wanted you here. After you left your interview, the Old Man said, 'He's one of us; he's a teacher.' "

This woman has pissed me off for most of the year, but I really appreciate this. It's just so rare to have somebody tell you that you're good at your job, much less that they can tell just by talking to you that you have teaching in your blood. It's a vote of confidence and a very nice way for the year to end.

But not as nice as another party at Al's house, which does happen, and which is fun in a kind of subdued way. Apparently this was a tough year for everybody. While everybody talks about how people were guzzling tequila in the pool until 3 A.M. last year, this year the party's mood is pretty well established when Chip, the principal, comes in at about five, sits down on the grass, and falls fast asleep until seven. Still, the food and company are great, and there is something very nice about ending the year here, where it began.

48

AND THE NEXT year begins similarly well. There are more meetings with the new transition department (it's actually the same, except, with Jessie gone, I'm teaching both sections of transition English this year), but since we did orientation last year, it is less painful to plan everything this year. The same stupid scheduling thing has happened again, where we have faculty orientation and student orientation at the same time, and once again the faculty orientation is a complete waste of time—you know, we have meetings where we sit around and talk about what the mission means to us, and although I am a proud pin wearer, the mission frankly doesn't mean shit to me; I only want to teach English.

But then, after the pre-freshmen are gone, the entire faculty gets on a bus to New Hampshire to go to this big retreat-type thingy with a high-ropes course and that kind of thing, so we can build our teamwork skills.

And while I think that the Nalgene-bottle-carrying crew (which constitutes about two thirds of the Better Than You faculty) tremendously overstates the team-building and self-esteem-building importance of a high-ropes course, and while I don't really think climbing a rickety structure in a stupid, testicle-crunching harness is a metaphor for anything, I am game to try anyway. I hope to God it's not a metaphor, because we go off to do our stupid activity, and it's a partners thing, and nobody picks me for their partner. I feel like I'm back in the second grade and nobody's picking me for the kickball team at recess just because I can't kick, run, or catch. So that kind of sucks, but I do eventually get up on the ropes, and it's fine, and then we break into department groups to try to build a raft to race around the pond, and this is actually a lot of fun, partly because the science department designs such a shitty raft that it falls apart as soon as it hits the water, and they all get soaked. English does respectably, but only because we have the office manager on our team to design a functional raft. During this exercise, I manage to scare the shit out of two new teachers by talking about how much Kathleen pissed me off, and I guess I sound pretty angry, so I come across as this scary, bitter fuck, which I guess is at least partially true, except for the scary part.

After all the metaphorical bonding experiences are finished, we drink beer and play Frisbee and eat, and it is just a great time. The vibe is really relaxed, and it feels totally different from last year, but in a good way. There is no longer the tension of Kathleen intimidating everybody, of Wilhelmina reproaching everybody, and once again, I am really proud and happy to work with such a cool bunch of people. There follows another big party at Al's house a few days later, and this is great too.

I call Jessie up, and she asks how school is going. "Well," I say, "you know that Spin Doctors song that starts out with 'Been a whole lot easier since the bitch is gone'? I kind of can't get that out of my head these days."

It gets harder much quicker, because my entire world falls apart on the second day of school when my wife, Kirsten, is diagnosed with breast cancer. I have already written a book about what this does to most of my life, but what it does to my teaching is, I think, to make it better. Or at least to make me appreciate it even more.

Partially this is because I am now doing my second run-through of the ninth-grade curriculum, so it's easier, but also it's just that I have come to really treasure all the time I spend here, because even given the unpredictability of teenagers, what happens here is something I'm used to, something I'm good at, and something I enjoy. Whereas being a cancer spouse is not something that I'm used to or good at, and it damn sure isn't any fun.

My advisory is back, minus two, and I find myself delighted to see them. To my amazement, Diana, the girl who was suspended fourteen times last year, is now bugging other people about their grades, organizing stuff, and impressing the hell out of me with her maturity. I don't know what happened over the summer, but I am psyched.

She invites me to her sweet-sixteen party, and because I got to know her better than anyone else last year due to all the meetings and conversations we had, and because I feel kind of parental toward all of my advisees, but especially her because of all the suspensions, I decide to go. It's kind of awkward at first, hanging out with my advisory in a social situation with no other adults I know around, but it's basically okay. The event is at some Polish social club in the hall on the second floor. On the first floor they have a bar. Early in the evening, while we're standing on the street, a guy staggers out of the bar, completely shitfaced. Ralph, one of my advisees, makes somebody take a picture with me, Ralph, and the drunk guy, who doesn't even seem to know what happens. The drunk guy staggers a few steps down the street, then falls. I run into the bar and say to the bartender, "Hey, that guy who just left is lying on the sidewalk out there, he's, like, so drunk he can't walk, do you think you could call him a taxi or something?"

The guy looks at me like I'm both annoying and stupid and offers the really spectacular non sequitur, "That guy's not Polish," before walking down to the end of the bar. When I go back outside, the non-Polish guy (who, by the way, spoke no English and was babbling in an obviously Slavic tongue, but, okay, whatever, isn't Polish) has managed to get about three blocks down the road under his own power.

Inside, I sit at a table between Will and Ralph, and we start making jokes about how Diana and her attendants are really, really late, and when a bunch of Diana's relatives bring in trays of food that are meant for after the birthday girl arrives, Ralph and Will start to goad each other into stealing a plate and bringing it back to the table, and I alternate between wanting to encourage them and feeling a responsibility to be an authority figure, so I smile and say nothing.

When the birthday party finally arrives, I find myself moved by an almost parental pride as boys and girls that I've only ever seen in the school uniform of a white shirt and dark pants proceed in slowly wearing poofy dresses and tuxedos. But it's getting late, and after wishing Diana a happy birthday, I sneak off as Will, Ralph, and everybody else heads for the food. It has been fun to see my advisees in this non-school situation, and as much as I have liked students at other schools, I just never would have gone to something like this even if I'd been invited. It would have seemed weird, but now it just feels like the right thing to do.

So that's fun, and the advisory, though two members still hate each other because of somebody's boyfriend two years ago, gets a lot mellower, and I really enjoy hanging out with them. We are even able to have conversations sometimes, which is remarkable. When it's our turn to present a town-meeting topic, we present the idea that town meeting should be renamed "assembly," because town meeting is a decision-making body, and this is just, well, an assembly. I think it gets voted down, but nobody cares about anything that happens in town meeting anyway. Last year I used to get really annoyed because some of the boys in my advisory would sit there and act like total jackasses throughout the whole thing, but I am slowly coming around to their point of view about the importance of this time.

They throw me a little birthday party in November, and I am really touched, especially remembering the way they hardly acknowledged my existence (in Denise's case literally) at the beginning of last year.

So it is a constant comfort to see these kids first thing in the morning, and to think about their problems in math or science or whatever as opposed to my problems. At the end of the year, somebody has screwed up the calendar and not built in any snow days (a really dumb mistake to make in Massachusetts), so we have to have two days of school after grades are in and exams are done. School must be open for four hours to satisfy the state, even though we have no classes. Instead we hang out in advisory groups. I bring my PlayStation, and we sit in the basement room playing video games, which certainly takes the sting out of having to have these two ridiculous days. In fact, it's really fun.

49

WITH KIRSTEN IN and out of the hospital for cancer treatment, I go through most of my days in a fear- and sleep-deprivation-induced fog, but I manage to do a pretty good job with my classes. It quickly becomes clear that one of my two English classes is "the loud class" and the other is "the quiet class," and this is how we refer to them in transition meetings for the rest of the year. I can't believe how much work we can get done in the quiet class—how awesomely cooperative they are, what great work they do. It's fantastic.

The loud class, on the other hand, is frequently derailed by the ever-shifting social politics of five girls—sometimes it's four against one, sometimes it's three against two, but there's always some sort of problem, and none of these girls are shy about stopping class right in the middle to yell across the room, "I hear what you're saying over there, and you better shut up, 'cause you run your mouth too much, you're gonna get slapped!" This leads, predictably, to "No, you better shut up, why don't you mind your business?" And so on. While it is kind of interesting to see how two girls who were allies yesterday could be yelling this at each other today (and then be allies again the day after that), it does kind of suck. In fact, there are many days when I feel like it's the quiet class that keeps me from feeling like I'm not cut out for this work. I mean, we do get stuff done in the loud class, but we are three days to a week behind the other class for the whole year because I just can't get them to stop yelling at each other.

In early October the transition department takes both classes to a high-ropes course for a beautiful team-bonding, metaphor-for-life experience. It ends up sucking horribly—it is poorly planned, and they have us doing these really hard activities: one is this thing where you have to climb up a phone pole and then jump off, trusting the people on the ground to pull hard enough on the rope attached to your harness that you won't splat on the ground. Several kids cry. On top of this, one of the counselors is terribly inappropriate—he doesn't seem to realize that he's the authority here, so he acts like one of the kids, wrestling with the boys, flirting with the girls, teasing Talia about her mustache, and, when Shakila refuses to climb the phone pole, he gets in her face and screams, "That's bullshit! Everybody climbs!" To her credit, Shakila does what I am too chickenshit to do—she yells back at the guy before running off to cry.

I just stand there dumbfounded and never speak up when this guy behaves so inappropriately. I have all kinds of justifications for this—we're in this weird situation off in the woods where we are depending on this guy, so I'm intimidated; he makes some speech at the beginning about how the fact that he is black means that he is uniquely qualified to work with these students, so then challenging him would set up an uncomfortable racial dynamic in addition to the uncomfortable "challenging the authority" dynamic, but this is a complete failure on my part to stand up and do what's right. I pride myself on having all this affection for the kids, but when it comes to having to do something really awkward and difficult in order to protect them, I drop the ball.

Anyway, the kids bounce back from this experience very quickly, and the people who run the place eventually give us a free return trip (but not, unfortunately, our money back) after Lisa, the study-skills teacher and organizer of the trip, complains in writing and via phone calls about how inappropriate and horrible the whole thing was.

Soon after this, we do our big October parent thing, and this time I decide that we should do scenes from *Romeo and Juliet,* so we perform them at night in the auditorium. Many people forget their lines, but it ends up being a pretty big success, for much the same reason that last year's trial of George was a success. One immediate effect is that a girl who had previously been very quiet and shy suddenly comes out of her shell the very day after the performances. This is great, except that it's not long before she joins in on the screaming across the room in the loud class. D'oh.

Overall, though, I follow the same curriculum as last year, so that's easier, and the quiet class continues to have a rare and perfect balance of personalities, so that, for example, Jack, who is a very young ninth-grader who seems to be popping out of his seat every ten seconds to do something goofy, never really gets out of hand here because he looks up to Kadeem, who is not only very cool but also very smart and serious and who can do more for Jack's behavior with one disapproving look than I can by talking to him for an hour.

Every year every English student at Better Than You has to pass a writing exam in order to be promoted to the next grade, and my quiet class becomes the only English class in the history of the school in which every student passes the writing exam on the first try. I would love to say that this is due to my incredible teaching skills—I mean, I would *really* love to be able to say that—but I have the loud class and their much lower initial passing rate to keep me humble. The fact is that a lot of what happens in the classroom just depends on the chemistry of the group that gets thrown together, and with this group, we got very lucky.

Even the loud class, though, ends up doing two more weeks of work (enough time to, grudgingly, do a half-assed job of *Julius Caesar*, so now I can say I did it and I'm a team player, though it still sucks and bores the hell out of both classes) than last year's class, which I really can't figure. I guess that it's partially due to me not floundering as much and just moving confidently from one thing to the next, skipping stuff that doesn't work, and knowing where to focus my energy. Or maybe it's just luck. Who knows.

At the end of every day, Lisa runs a knitting elective in my classroom, and while Kirsten is in the hospital, I always end up coming back from my daily visit during this class. It's mostly kids I've taught before, and everybody is just really nice to me when I walk in, and Lisa and a few of her students are among the very few people (Alison and Sydney from the transition department are others) who get the joke and agree to take the CHEMOTHERAPY stickers from the roll I steal from Kirsten's hospital room. There is a great feeling here, and partially it's because Lisa is running a very relaxed class teaching something she loves, but I also just really appreciate the low-key kindness I get from the students every day. I'm not always in the best mental shape when I come back from the hospital, and coming in here with these kids always reminds me why I like working here, how much I like the kids, and how being a teacher is as beneficial to me as it is to my students. If not, you know, more.

Apart from my classes and my advisory going well, random kids and adults throughout the school have been really nice to me. I expect it from the adults, but I'm surprised at how much I get it from the kids. One kid I know only from having proctored his study hall in the first trimester of last year will periodically stop and ask, "How's your wife?" I always appreciate this even if I don't have anything new to say.

So at the end of the year, as we're wrapping it all up and having our final town meeting, I ask Chip if I can speak. I get up (to wild cheers led by my advisory, which I am not above loving for shameful, egotistical reasons) and say, "Back in October, I was supposed to lead an inspirational moment at town meeting, but I, well, I blew it off, because I wasn't feeling very inspirational at the time. Actually, it was about all I could do to get out of bed. As many of you know, my wife was diagnosed with breast cancer this year. She had a really punishing treatment that required her to be in the hospital for six weeks in December and January, including Christmas. So it's been a really tough year for me and my family, but one of the things that has really helped me has been all of the love and support I have gotten from my coworkers, my students, my advisory, and the whole Better Than You Community. So I just wanted to thank you for all of your support this year. I also want to let you know that my wife recently had a scan, and there is currently no trace of cancer in her body. Thank you."

Everybody applauds, and I feel incredibly grateful to be a part of a place like this. Yes, there are a lot of things that are fucked up, but, fucked up or not, this place is a community in a way that no other workplace I've ever been in can touch.

50

UNFORTUNATELY, THERE ARE storm clouds on the horizon. Back in January of this same year, I take a day off when Kirsten comes out of the hospital, and I miss all kinds of drama when Rachael, our invisible cofounder, comes in and tells everybody how the board has decided that we need a superintendent. As a charter school, we are legally a school district as well as just a school, and so Chip, our principal, has to do all the reporting-this-and-that-and-the-other-thing-to-the-state paperwork that a superintendent of schools does for a school district as well as all the running-the-school stuff that a principal does for a school. According to Rachael and Chip, Chip can't really do both jobs, so we need a superintendent to take over those duties. Only, you know, we are an innovative charter school, so we're going to call him a president.

It's adding a layer of bureaucracy, but more than that, it's changing the supposed focus of the school, because no superintendent is going to be content with just doing paperwork for the state and raising money; a superintendent will want to run things. Superintendents want to issue pointless orders and start bogus "initiatives," like the Tight-Panted Southerner Education System training I did at Northton. This is how they justify their salaries and prove they are in charge. Only *we* are supposed to be in charge. Right? I mean, isn't that the whole point of this school? I can't tell if this is a terrible failure of imagination and heart or a carefully planned evil plot cooked up by Rachael to wreck the vision of the school. I try to believe it's the former, but our next meeting on this topic gives me a strange sense that the evil-plot theory is closer to the truth.

In February Rachael comes back, but this time she brings Spencer Hackington, who is on our board and whose big claim to fame is that he's a serial political appointee. He keeps getting Republicans to appoint him to run stuff—state agencies, city departments—and I wonder how, aside from obviously kissing a serious amount of ass, one gets into the political-appointee business. It seems, to judge by Mr. Hackington's record, to be a pretty sweet gig.

Anyway, as you would expect of a guy who is used to running stuff (and who is picked by the party hostile to government employees to oversee government employees), this guy is a total asshole, and he spends the meeting yelling at us and belittling our concerns. This is really not a good sign. I state my concern about how the priorities of a superintendent are frequently at odds with those of teachers, and how I am afraid that having a superintendent—oh, sorry, president— is going to mean that teachers' priorities will be sacrificed.

To his credit, Hackington doesn't really dispute my point or my conclusion—he just points to a chart he has about how much money needs to be raised for the school to grow. Ugh.

So we are all feeling kind of queasy about what the board is doing, and this is doubly troubling because the board is chaired by Rachael, who lives in New York, and otherwise consists of people who never set foot in the place. They also do all kinds of sleazy maneuvers like going into executive session for two hours, then opening the doors at 10 P.M. so that the vote they are taking about the direction of the school can be, as required by law, "public."

Almost the entire faculty starts having secret meetings, and we draft a no-confidence motion, and a bunch of teachers go to a board meeting and read it, and it feels really great—we all get together to fight the power, and then we actually do something rather than just talking about it. Though what we really should be doing is starting a union, but many of my colleagues have been brainwashed by the whole idea of the "charter school movement," which is something we hear about a lot around here. It's this idea that charter schools all over the country represent a revolution in public education, that these small, nimble start-ups are the future and big behemoth "regular public schools" (a derogatory term here in the halls of Better Than You) with unions are the past. So many of my colleagues, because this is the only place they've ever worked, believe, despite their own long hours, inequitable class assignments, and substandard pay and benefits, that unions are the embodiment of evil. It's pretty clear to me that Rachael and Hackington are the embodiment of evil, and that a union would help us have a voice in decisions that are going to affect us, but most of my colleagues aren't buying. Lisa tries to start the union-election process and gets a whopping six signatures.

So that's bad. Also bad is that somehow this clandestine fight-the-power stuff has gotten linked to "diversity" stuff, and that we can only have one if we have the other, and we have to talk about "these issues" if we are going to really work together. It's not exactly clear to me what "these issues" are. I know that there is a history of racial tension here, that the departure of the African-American principal added to the tension, and people are always saying how all the "staff of color" leave, though from what I can see, the staff of whiteness pretty much do too, but okay, all the people who've been here since the beginning, or even any longer than me, except for one, are white, and maybe this is not as warm and fuzzy and loving a community for everybody as I think it is. And clearly the departure of Kathleen and Wilhelmina hasn't actually helped.

So we meet once to discuss this stuff, and it mostly consists of people talking about their pain, and nobody is really talking about much of anything work-related except for the occasional vague, accusatory reference to "some people," until Trish, our college counselor, starts crying and says that none of her colleagues ever come to talk to her. The meeting breaks up not long after that, and I'm feeling dubious about this whole process, and then we have another meeting, and we have no process or facilitator or anything, and

Trish starts yelling about how some Jewish teacher in New York just did something horrible to some black kids, and some Jewish staff ask why it always has to be about Jews, and Erik, the vice principal, says that he is really outraged because the students in town meeting voted down a resolution favoring reparations for slavery, and this really shows that we have a lot of work to do, and that we are really damaging these kids. (I think it has more to do with the fact that nobody pays the slightest attention to anything that happens in town meeting and that most of our black students are of Jamaican, Haitian, or Trinidadian ancestry, and might perhaps have different feelings on this issue from students whose ancestors were enslaved in the United States.) Roberta tries to disagree with Erik, and she is shut down by Trish, who is screaming, tears in her eyes, that Erik is a black man and we must show him deference.

That pretty well kills the meeting, and I go down to the basement as angry as I've ever been at work. I am literally throwing stuff across my classroom, because my feelings are hurt. Because, if I understand Trish correctly, my job as a white man in this school is to shut up and take orders from the black people. Because I have to sit through these bullshit meetings and listen to people prattle on about their pain. Because my presence here somehow makes me suspect. The fact that I live in the city and work in the city and grew up in the city means nothing—the fact that I am white in this place means that I have to get a big ration of shit because of my skin color. Well, hooray for diversity.

I rant to a couple of people I trust about this, and one of them runs back to Trish and tells her everything I said. I have no idea why. I feel like I'm in the seventh grade. I send an e-mail to the entire staff saying that I am through having these conversations without a facilitator because I don't want to be yelled at. I get a raft of responses about what an evil reactionary I am, and how this school is not ready for "this work." I end up having coffee with Trish one day to try to smooth things over. Trying as hard as possible to be politically correct and using lots of "I statements," I say that *I* felt anger in the meeting when Trish was screaming at us because *I* recall how, in *my* family, when someone is yelling at you, they want you to shut up, that to *me*, yelling like that is a way of ending a discussion, not starting one.

Trish is also hip to the I statements, so she informs me that in *her* family, yelling at people is just the way they have conversations, which makes me damn glad I didn't grow up in her house. I say how I understood her to be saying that she thought that the white staff should pretty much shut up and let the black staff tell us what to do, and while we do end up having a cordial coffee, she never really tells me that I misinterpreted her.

The diversity committee ends up hiring some diversity consultants to help us "do this work" (what is the work? What is the goal? Nobody can tell me) next year, so the whole thing dies down, and the next thing we know we get a letter from Rachael saying that the two finalists for the president position are Trish and Brian Watkins, the principal who got me my first interview with the fingernail lady at Court Street.

We all talk feverishly about this for weeks, and the faculty decides that we favor Trish. Trish has done a top-notch job as the college counselor and has tons of experience, and Watkins is a guy who goes into failing schools and kicks asses and takes names. Parents and teachers go to interviews with both Trish and Watkins, and everybody agrees that Trish gives a much better interview, she knows the school and has ideas about it, whereas Watkins just talks about how great he is, sometimes even using the third person, like he's James Brown or something.

It should go without saying that Watkins is the one who gets hired. We, including Trish, find this out by seeing an article in the paper that comes out on graduation day. It has Watkins' smiling face, and a big, laudatory article about what a great job he did at his old school, and how he is excited to lead this new school, especially because he doesn't have the constraints of a union.

We're all pretty outraged and demand a meeting, and they trot out Spencer Hackington again, and he says, yes, it's a terrible shame that the paper knew before Trish did, that she had to find out from the sound guy at graduation, but that we have no way of knowing who planted that article, a lot of people are mad at him for leaving the Boston Public Schools, any of them could have dropped a dime, et cetera. It's probably pretty unlikely that Watkins' enemies got this fawning story printed, but I guess anything is possible.

So as the year ends, I am, as I say to the kids, feeling incredibly happy to work here, really warm and loving about the entire community, but I am also scared about both the racial fault lines in the faculty and the turmoil I know is coming next year.

And the two feelings are intertwined—because we all work so hard and so closely together, and because the school is still, after seven years, a kind of new thing, a work in progress, I have felt supported by a community here in a way I never did before. We are, after all and despite our differences, united in the belief that we are part of something important and that we get to build it. But because we all work so hard and so closely together, and because the school is so new, there is no culture or structure to insulate me from administrative turmoil. The principal and vice principal were new in my second year of Northton, but I was far enough down the food chain at a thousand-student high school that it didn't really affect me much. Here, though, if there is a shit storm at the top, we're all going to get dirty.

51

THE NEW REGIME does not begin well. I stop in before the school year starts, and Roberta, who is now the lead teacher of English, explains how we now have eight administrators. In a school with two hundred students. There is the president, of course, and then the president's assistant, who is his secretary that has worked with him for seventeen years. Then there is the president's assistant for parent and community relations. She has also been with the president for seventeen years. Then there is the vice president. This, in a master stroke of political genius, is Trish. So rather than having her just running around perhaps attracting her own power base, a shadow presidency, Watkins has co-opted her. Fantastic. There are also now four "deans": the vice principal, the head of special ed, a new "dean of history, science, and eleventh and twelfth grade," and a new "dean of math, English, and ninth and tenth grade." We seem to have a dean for just about everything now, so I ask which one is the dean of my left one. Nobody can ever tell me.

Significantly, what's missing here is a full-time college counselor. If Trish isn't doing it and nobody's replaced her, then what exactly are we going to do about getting these kids into college? Apparently this will be another responsibility of the dean of history, science, and eleventh and twelfth grade, who just happens to be another Watkins crony from his former school.

Then Roberta informs me that we are going to have several days of mandatory training at the beginning of the year from the Buzzword Institute. Now, starting the year with mandatory staff "training" is bad enough, but we had the head of the Buzzword Institute here last year, and he was slick and insulting and such an asshole that I walked out of his presentation, marking the second time I had ever walked out of a meeting. Apparently he is a good buddy of Watkins, so the Buzzword Institute has landed a cool twenty-five-thousand-dollar contract to "train" us this year. I'm thinking we could have probably bought half a college counselor for that.

So I am already feeling a little nervous and desperate, but then something weird and wonderful happens. I run into Gordon Stevens, my old mentor and professional hero, in the hallway here at Better Than You. It seems like divine intervention. We have a nice conversation—he is now mostly out of the classroom and doing some kind of work training teachers for the district and kind of getting ready to retire. He tells me nice things about how much he enjoyed working with me, and he says of Watkins, whom he has worked with (though not under), "He's good, because you can argue with him and he'll listen to you. He won't always agree, but he does listen." I reserve judgment about that, but overall, it's tremendously rejuvenating to see this guy. See! He's been at it for close to thirty years! And he's still as smart and committed as ever! And he believes in me! Maybe I can keep doing this.

Then I see the president's assistant in the hallway, and she says, "I saw you talking to Dr. Stevens."

"Yeah," I say, "I did my student teaching under him. He taught me everything I know."

"He's been working with *us*, you know. He was here to see Dr. Watkins."

"Uhhh, yeah, that's what he said."

"Yes. He was here for *us*."

Okay then! This is so weird. It's like my having a freaking conversation with this guy was some kind of threat, and this woman felt like she had to assert that the encounter didn't really belong to me—it was just an unfortunate by-product of Dr. Watkins' encounter.

Now it's time for us to have our big beginning-of-the-year meeting with the Big Man himself.

The day starts pretty much like most first days of school in most regular schools, which is what this is now. The superintendent—sorry, president—is here to tell us about his vision, our mission, and stuff like that.

Only, of course, this meeting, unlike the ones at Northton, will not have our union president telling us how many days till the first day off, ha-ha (this is the only real innovation).

He begins by bullying us—write down the number between one

and ten that shows how much you want this school to succeed, write down yes or no to "are you willing to work hard," blah blah blah. It's standard education-administrator bullshit and therefore really nothing to worry about, but it makes me angry and sad. First of all, this guy just walked in here and is asking me to quantify my commitment to the job I've been doing for two years. Like he's the one who cares, and we're the ones who need to be whipped into shape. Second, for all its flaws, this used to be our school.

Now it's his school. What the hell, he's probably better at running it than we were. In the end maybe it will be a good thing, but, you know, I'm standing here watching the dream of a school in which teachers make important decisions dying in front of my eyes. Maybe it was too weak to live—it's pretty clear now that Rachael never believed in it, and Kathleen bailed out before it came down to fighting for it—but I miss it. I hate to see it go.

But the Watkins show gets better as it goes along. He lays off the bullying tone and asks for questions, which he then doesn't answer— most notably, what we are going to do about the fact that we have twice as many seniors as last year, and essentially no real college counselor. He answers that one with, "What did you personally do to help students get into college last year? You'll just have to keep doing that!" I wonder how his vice president might feel about the implication that she basically did nothing last year as the college counselor. Still, he gets more and more charming as the time goes by, and by the third hour, we are all eating out of his hand. Me included. I am ready to dance on the grave of the vision of this school if I can only be allowed to work for this wonderful man.

He's got skills. He's very charming, he makes us laugh, and he probably hits the favorite button of everyone in the room at least once. For me it's when he pooh-poohs all of our diversity efforts. The president informs us that we have lots of rules written down about appropriate communication, and that we should address the problem of people breaking the rules. But why should we take up everybody else's time with this? It would sure be nice if we all worked out our issues and everything, but how can that compare with serving the kids as a focus for our time?

Like I said, I am eating out of his hand.

So much that I forget his weird, non sequitur answer about the college counselor, and the fact that this means that I as a senior advisor will have to step in and do this college counseling I'm not trained for, and my advisees will suffer as a result, and if I complain about the workload, I am not a team player willing to do whatever it takes for these kids. I will also forget what it says about his priorities that having all these cronies on the payroll trumps having a college counselor.

Well, we'll see. Like I said, I have seen a lot of these meetings. At Newcastle, and then for the first couple of years at Northton, they always scared the shit out of me, because administrators just love to talk about their new initiatives and programs and ideas and I always got intimidated by this stuff until I realized that it very rarely has any real impact on what happens in my room. Basically if you're doing your job, you're okay. Actually in most schools you're okay even if you're not doing your job.

At the end of the day we go for our picnic/barbecue. It's not at Al's house. They say this is because we should be partying in the city we serve instead of the suburb where Al lives, but I think Al being the official party guy gives him a power that is threatening to the new folks. So we go to Franklin Park, which is a spot I actually love to walk and bike through, but we are in perhaps the very shittiest, most depressing part of the park—a sad cluster of picnic tables between a busy road and some tennis courts, and sitting in the shadow of a giant public hospital. It is a pathetic, desultory affair. In years past these events were real parties. At least, they were to me. They really felt like family get-togethers, only without the weird, forty-year-old resentments about who told Grandma when Aunt Betty ate too many cookies.

Of course, some people never came to these things and apparently always felt excluded, and yes, this always included most of the staff "of color," so maybe my warm fuzzy idea of what this place was was a lie all along.

In any case, this shitty picnic grove has no place to pee, thus guaranteeing that nobody can really stay that long. There are tubs of catered crap from some barbecue joint that I guess is good if you eat meat but sucks hard-core if you don't because they even put meat in the vegetables, so the food right away sends me the message that my dietary needs (no meat—doesn't seem too extreme to me) are freakish and won't be catered to. We sit around for an hour and a half having a pale imitation of fun. Some people throw a Frisbee. I wish I'd stayed home. Next time I will. If there is a next time. After all, this isn't a family, and it isn't even any kind of special new vision or anything like that.

It's just another school.

5 2

I SPEND THREE days with my departments working on curriculum, improving stuff that works, junking stuff that doesn't. Nobody notices or says anything.

I, along with the rest of the transition department—Alison, Lisa, Hillary, a new math teacher, and Dinah, a new English teacher—plan ninth-grade orientation. It goes smoother than it ever has, except for the fact that Erik, the vice princ—I mean Dean of Yelling at Kids—is supposed to give out lockers and falls way behind and refuses to accept any help when Alison offers, so we have to send twenty kids home without lockers. The best part of the orientation is that some of our older students are here pitching in, and they are doing a fantastic job—they are helpful and mature and kind to the terrified ninth-graders. One senior—actually the same kid from my study hall who always asked after Kirsten's health last year—says, "I'm just going to imagine that every one of these ninth-graders is my little brother." We're all unspeakably proud of them. No administrator notices or says anything.

Everybody else is in the Buzzword Institute training. It's scheduled for ten hours over two days. Those of us who oversaw ninth-grade orientation come in three hours late, so we only get seven hours of training. The people doing schedules and computer setup are not excused, so they will have to work over Labor Day weekend in order to get this stuff ready for school. We all have rooms to set up, syllabuses to write, and classes to get in order, but we are not allowed to do any of that stuff here on the last two days before kids come in to school.

Now, the training is pretty typical. There is a glib guy—thankfully not the same asshole from last year but pretty much cut from the same cloth—with a strangely hostile undercurrent and an utterly typical condescending undercurrent who shows us lots of fancy PowerPoint slides about his company's idea to revolutionize education, which they are doing because they care so much, and the twenty-five thousand dollars we're paying them doesn't hurt either.

I won't bore you with any of the details—it's bad enough that I have to suffer through this. None of the ideas are anything you could really argue with, though of course everything is oversimplified.

What I will tell you is that our glib, hostile, condescending presenter has never been a high school teacher.

Now, it's demoralizing enough to be sitting here listening to ten hours of this guy's system—oh, what the hell, I'll tell you for free: all kids can learn, and you should make decisions about what you are doing based on data. If you happen to be a school superintendent, I will happily come and deliver this message to your staff in five minutes for only $12,500—please contact me care of my publisher—but it is just crushing to know that this guy is not now, nor has he ever been, a teacher.

Probably he calls himself an "educator." It's hard for me to think of another profession where people are forced to have someone who's never done their job tell them how to do their job. I mean, just imagine doctors going to a conference to get surgical instruction from a nonsurgeon. Or Mark McGwire being forced to take hitting instruction from George Will.

Now, I don't mean to suggest that I am the Mark McGwire of teachers, but I like to think I am at least a valuable everyday player with a pretty high batting average and solid defensive skills, not the kind of guy who makes the cover of *Sports Illustrated* very much, but the kind of guy who plays every day and is not a liability in the field or behind the plate. And this unctuous, car-salesmany guy is telling me how to do my job. I used to think the old people at Northton were cranky freaks for hating our department head there just because she had never been a high school English teacher (though at least, unlike this guy, she had been *some* kind of teacher), but now, after eight years, I get it. It sucks.

Anyway, the unctuous car salesman gives us all these books of photocopies of the same stuff that's on his PowerPoint slides. On the first day, I leave my book on my desk, because my desk is in the meeting room. The next day it's gone.

So I'm sitting there with no book giving off sullen vibes (this has as much to do with the fact that Kirsten is in the hospital getting tests to see if her cancer has come back as it does with the fact that I am about to have five hours of my precious life wasted in this room), and the presenter comes over and says, "Brendan, do you have a book?"

What, do I work for him now?

"No, I left it on my desk and it was taken."

He comes back about thirty seconds later—it's now about a minute before we're supposed to start—with a book in his hand, and he says, "This one's mine, but you can go make a photocopy."

Now, this plan is predicated on the whole belief that it's important for us to have these books, which we did not use yesterday, and whose entire contents will be displayed on the screen for us in the five long hours we have ahead of us.

"Well, by the time I did sixty double-sided pages, I'd be really late—I'm just gonna look on with Lisa."

He leaves and comes back about ten seconds later with a smug look on his face and oozes, "Brian wants to see you." He just went and ratted me out to my boss! Unbelievable. Well, it's okay, I mean Brian has been a principal for a long time; he knows what's really important here, right?

I go over to see Brian, who is helping himself to a donut and talking to somebody else. When he sees me approaching, he stops his conversation and says, "Mr. Halpin, you need to have your book. Go photocopy that book right now."

This is the first thing beyond hello that the man has said to me in the week I've been working for him.

So I go up and make my photocopies and come in late in front of everybody and hand the book to the asshole who ratted me out, and I sit there for five hours and dutifully turn the pages in time with the PowerPoint slides and never need the book for anything.

Curriculum may or may not get done, the ninth grade may or may not be welcomed to the school, schedules may or may not be ready, but by God, I have my book, and that's what's really important.

53

THINGS PRETTY MUCH continue in this vein. I spend my morning commute on the first few days composing my resignation letter. Really. I know it needs to be a doozy, because our new president is such a skillful self-promoter that when we all leave at the end of this year (as I am increasingly sure a large number of us will), I am sure he will be able to paint it as a tremendous success on his part, because he managed to get rid of all of us who are dead weight, who are not with the program, who are not committed to devoting effective effort to finding effective practice to work toward the development of all students and, um, hitting our proficiency targets.

Sometimes the teachers play a game where we try to use all the buzzwords we can in one sentence. (I got four at the end of the last paragraph.) We also laugh about whether we are allowed to talk to each other. In the first few weeks of school, we keep getting e-mails telling us who we are not allowed to talk to. Teachers are not allowed to talk to anybody except lead teachers and deans. So, for example, if I am missing a bus pass for an advisee, I am not allowed to talk to the office manager who controls the bus passes. I must talk to my dean, who will talk to the office manager (no longer the fabulous, competent, kind woman who designed the English-department bonding raft but some cranky lady Watkins brought in). And, needless to say, my student won't get her bus pass.

I'm not sure if these policies are just supposed to humiliate us or if they actually have some purpose. In any case, we laugh bitterly about them all the time now. The office manager will come in to the teachers' room and ask somebody a question—apparently she's allowed to talk to us—and when she leaves the person will say, "Oh, was I allowed to talk to her?" and we all laugh, and somebody else asks if we are hitting our proficiency targets, and we all laugh. I tell my friends that if I can get through the entire year without grabbing my crotch in a meeting and saying, "I got your proficiency target right here," it will be something of a miracle.

On the second day of school we start getting "feedback visits." These, we are assured, are meant to support us. Of course, they are really spot checks to ensure compliance with all the new regulations that are in place supposedly to support student learning, but actually to separate the sheep from the goats, to tell who's on the team and who's not.

I quickly find myself becoming a goat. On the day after the World Trade Center horror, they tell us in an early-morning meeting that we should talk with our advisories about what happened, that we should just let it all hang out and let the discussion go where the students want it to. So on September 12 I am starting my free-for-all, let-it-all-hang-out discussion (and finding that I am way more freaked out by September 11 than my students are) and I get a visit from Erik, the Dean of Yelling at Kids, who my students all hate, who indeed has been the source of probably half the suspensions that my advisory has accumulated over the last two years, mostly for what he calls in his e-mails "insubordination to administrator," which includes at least one of my advisees calling him a "chump" to his face, which is something I only wish I had the guts to do, which is maybe why I love my advisory so much. Anyway, Erik is now nominally in charge of advisors for some reason, and he comes into my advisory here on September 12, when we had been told to have a lesson-plan-out-the-window kind of discussion (like any of us had a lesson plan in the first place), and my advisees, who had just been warming up to a conversation, clam up the way pretty much everybody does when somebody they hate is in the room. Later I get an e-mail from Erik telling me I should have had an objective on the board.

I have a class in which I plan to have a really quick, lame discussion about a summer-reading book that I think they haven't read, and the kids end up having a fantastic discussion that goes way beyond the lame thing I had planned. So my plans are out the window. One of the deans is watching the class. She sends me an e-mail telling me that I was ungrounded and should have the Massachusetts curriculum frameworks on the board.

The Massachusetts curriculum frameworks for English is a forty-five-page document. It is not clear exactly how I am to transcribe it in the five minutes between classes. Or should I just post it all?

So evidently the new regime is all about stuff on the board. Now this particular dean who told me to put the curriculum frameworks on the board is actually somebody I like and respect because of her work as a special-ed teacher here last year. Has she gone nuts trying to interpret strange orders from above? Or am I feeling so threatened that her feedback sounds more bizarre than it actually is? Or both?

One good thing does come of this—this fractious group of teachers that I feared could never work together after last year's diversity debacle is now, for the most part, incredibly tight-knit. We have a common enemy.

At the end of the third week, Chip sends out an e-mail thanking us for all we are doing right and saying he is going to make the deans back off for a week. It's nice, but it falls short of the actual apology we need. Nobody yet has acknowledged that we ever knew what we were doing, that we have been horribly insulted by this hounding "support." (Some genius went into somebody's class on the second day of school and observed cogently that she hadn't succeeded in building a rapport with the students yet.) Nobody has actually admitted that they made a mistake.

So we have a week of peace, and then it's back to spot checks to make sure we are doing all our busywork to appear to be with the program, it's back to the résumé polishing, and it's back to the sad, angry jokes in the teachers' room.

Brian Watkins has carefully nurtured a reputation as a genius school administrator because he has made a couple of disgraceful schools into respectably mediocre schools. I don't know about that, but I do know he has made this into an intolerable situation, and the grim camaraderie that comes with standing on the deck of a sinking

ship with people you like won't be enough to keep me afloat next
year.

54

HAT MAKES THE situation especially sad is that I'm really enjoying my classes this year. I am once again teaching two
sections of ninth-grade English, and my first-period class is just
fantastic. It's the kind of quick, lively, good-natured group that I
have had only two or three times in the last nine years. At the beginning of class, we write for two minutes nonstop, just to kind of
clear everybody's heads for the rest of the class, and I allow the kids
to share what they've written. In most classes, five or six kids will
share, but in this class everybody shares. All fifteen of them.

This really helps the class cohere and get to know each other in a
way that is rare and wonderful. So, for example, we hear all about
Patrice's meals from the night before—multicourse, mouthwater-
ing affairs described in loving detail and always finishing with what
flavor Kool-Aid was served. By November we are all joking that we
are going to show up on Patrice's doorstep on Thanksgiving. She
tells us we're not invited but acknowledges that there will probably
be enough food for us.

Pete is an aspiring poet and sometimes drops a new poem on us
during this time. Luke, who's Haitian, always begins his freewrite
with "Yo, yo, yo, yo, yo," which is especially funny to me because I
had a white kid about as different from Luke as two people can be
back in Northton who used to do the same thing. Talia is an aspiring rapper, and she spends the first several weeks sharing really
conventional gangsta-type stuff about spitting her rhyme and cap-
ping us with her nine, until the other students sort of peer-pressure

her into proving she can rhyme about something other than mur-
der. And Laxmi, who's dating Kadeem from last year's quiet class,
keeps us posted on the ups and downs of that relationship. So, for a
few months, several kids talk about how the class feels like a family,
and on Mondays half the class writes about how much they missed
everybody over the weekend.

It won't last, because Pete and Luke will have a falling-out, and
later, in February, three new students will join the class, changing
the dynamic quite significantly, but for the most part, the class is a
joy to teach.

My other section of ninth-graders is a lot more work. They are
suspicious and resistant—the "transition conversation" this year is
especially painful and turns into this running joke among the kids
about how they are stupid, which is exactly the kind of thing this
program was trying to avoid.

So if these kids are less sold on school, they are still a lot of fun to
work with. They crack me up every day, and I know I am not able to
be as firm with them as I should. The prime example of this comes
late in the year, when they start thinking it's really hilarious to say
"shiz-nit" all the time instead of "shit," and "biz-nitch" instead of
"bitch" because, you know, then they're not swearing, so it's okay to
say in class, right? So I manage to get them to stop with the biz-
nitch, but every day when I give homework, I get, "Now that's some
shiz-nit," or when I yell at Mario that he should actually read during
the silent reading time, he gives me "That's some shiz-nit." One day,
a kid is doing something he's not supposed to do, and he hasn't even
started on this big project due next week, so I gently remind him to
get to work, and he says, "Aw, that's some shiz-nit," and I reply with,
"No, what's some shiz-nit is that you have this project due next week
and you haven't even started it! *That's* some shiz-nit!"

This is probably not the best tack for me to take if I want to convince them that using modified swear words in class is, well, some
shiz-nit.

I am also teaching seniors for the first time since my first year at Northton, and it's proving to be kind of a mixed bag. I've known these kids for years now, and about half my advisory is in my class. I have these fantasies about all the great discussions we are going to have about all the fabulous literature we are going to read.

Unfortunately, it doesn't really play out that way. Mainly this is because most of the kids don't read the books. Now, this is not a new problem, and it's certainly not unique to these kids—indeed, I think it's probably the central problem of my entire academic discipline—but none of this makes it any easier to get stuff done. I always try to put the kids' ideas at the center of the class activities, but I can't really do that here because they don't really have any ideas because they haven't done the reading. So we have a lot of painfully slow days.

And since they are seniors, they are subject to senioritis, which means that these problems actually manage to get worse as the year goes along. But at the end of each trimester, with the closing-of-grades deadline looming, they turn into machines. They write and revise papers at an unbelievable clip, and most of them end up doing pretty well in the class, especially considering how little they've done for the rest of the trimester. Talking about this phenomenon with somebody, I have an epiphany—"It's like they do nothing for eight weeks, and then there's this two-week frenzy of activity . . . whoa. I guess maybe they are ready for college." Yes, they appear to have already mastered the collegiate "party, relax, party, relax, study" calendar. I think they'll probably do very well when they get to college.

Then there is my advisory itself. While it suffers the usual senior problems of chronic tardiness and low attendance, it becomes a real safe haven for me. I am not sure what the students get out of having me as an advisor, but I sure as hell get a lot out of having them as advisees.

The door is closed every morning so we can talk frankly, and almost all semblance of professional detachment is gone from my interactions with them. What I mean is that usually when kids are complaining about a teacher or something, I will keep my opinions to myself, even if I agree with them, which I usually do, because it just seems unprofessional to join in. And if I am having difficulties with the administration, I will usually try to keep that to myself, but here, with these kids, I find that I just can't put on that "Mr. Halpin" face for them. We know each other too well, and I really feel like they helped see me through the worst year of my life last year. So they complain about their "college counselor"; the dean who is handling college counseling on a part-time basis while she tries to do the rest of her job is, according to them, not doing this job anywhere near as well as Trish did with last year's seniors. (She's also been overheard telling one of her college-search groups, "Don't make Mommy angry," which is just creepy.) At first I try to equivocate a little bit and say that Mommy was set up to fail, but eventually I just more or less agree and tell them that I think they've been screwed over by the school. Those who have another English teacher complain that their English class is boring (those who have me probably think the same thing but are kind enough to keep it to themselves), and I allow as how, yeah, the one I sat in on was pretty boring, but that's no excuse for you to be asleep, don't you think I have to sit through some boring meetings, and you don't see me falling asleep, I'd be fired in a minute if I did.

Which might not be so bad, except that I really want to see these kids graduate. It's the main reason I didn't just walk out the door when Dr. Watkins said that anybody who wasn't willing to give 110 percent should walk out the door. Or at any number of other points. I bring this up all the time with my colleagues—mostly the four teachers I share this basement room with. (Everybody else keeps moving out of this room, but I stay because it's far away from the office on the second floor and all the gossip and drama that goes on up there, and this year it is really a fantastic sanctuary, and I really like sharing the room with Hillary, Michelle, and Carol, who are all new this year.)

"I just need to hang on till June and see them across the stage," I say, and eventually I end up saying something like this to the advisory when they are complaining about how the school is fucked in some way, or some person is pissing them off, or whatever. "Let's just focus on graduation. Whatever your problems here, you have something you want to get out of this situation, so let's focus on getting there, and then, at the end of June, we'll all walk out of this place together." This is quite early in the year, and way before I have made my decision to leave this place official. It never hits the school rumor mill, which I take, rightly or not, as a nice example of the trust that's built up between us.

55

AT NORTHTON WHEN I was sick and tired of all the bitter old fucks I worked with, I wondered how they got that way. I used to ask Terri this because she wasn't a bitter old fuck, but she started teaching there at the same time they did. They would occasionally tell stories about those days—they all used to room together and go out together, and somehow these cranky old fifty-five-year-olds were once fun-loving twenty-three-year-olds. It seemed impossible at the time.

Terri would try to explain. She would talk about strikes and the bitterness they engendered, about years of persistent disrespect from various school administrations. She had come to the conclusion that the Northton administration was, in fact, not evil but just dangerously stupid, and that their incredible disrespect for their staff was to blame for the staff becoming bitter old fucks.

I would listen and think, yeah, well, whatever. The past is the past. Move on already.

And today I sit in a department meeting as Roberta relays the latest evil and/or stupid dictates from the administration, and when I am not declaiming about their stupidity or evil, I am interjecting shitty little comments. For example, Roberta tells us we will all need to spend our department-meeting time being trained in the ATLAS protocol of looking at student work.

Now, I don't know shit about the ATLAS protocol. It may well be the best thing since sliced bread. But I feel compelled to mock it because we used to be able to set our own agendas, and in fact we have a lot of legitimate stuff we want to work on this year, and here's the administration jumping in and telling us not only are we not allowed to set our own priorities for the department anymore (remember, this school was supposedly founded on the principle that teachers set the priorities for the *school*), but we don't know how to look at student work together. And, frankly, anything that's coming from them, after our horrible time with the Buzzword Institute, is suspect.

So I make some shitty comment, like "That's sure to be a good and valuable use of my time."

And I look across the table at Julie. Julie is new this year, and this is her third year of teaching. I find her kind of suspect because she was brought in by the hated new administration from their previous school, just as the bitter fucks at Northton found me suspect because I was hired by an administration they hated. In my mind, I have given her provisional "one of us" status, but I haven't blocked out the possibility that she's "one of them."

And she gives me this look that says, "How did this guy get to be so incredibly tiresome? How did bitterness become his overriding emotion?" And because my negativity pisses her off the way negativity used to piss me off, she takes a thinly veiled potshot at me:

"We actually used the ATLAS protocol a lot last year, and no matter how great you think you are, you can still learn something from it."

So here I am, the bitter old fuck that the new teachers in their twenties hate. And I want to explain, explain about the dream that existed here of a place where teachers mattered and how hard it is to watch it die, explain how hard it is to be disrespected when you've got what you think is a fair amount of expertise under your belt, how degrading it is to sit in these trainings with condescending nonteachers who say things like "If you decide to make a commitment to these kids" when we work with kids and these assholes just fly around the country boring and insulting people with PowerPoint presentations. I never wanted to end up like this.

I would say this is the fate of all teachers, but I know from working with Gordon Stevens, from working with Terri, that it doesn't have to be this way, that there is a way to get old in this profession without getting to be a tiresome, bitter old fuck.

I guess I just don't know what it is yet.

In the meantime, I will continue to be a bitter old fuck. But I'll have plenty of company, as just about every day somebody is upset or outraged about something, whether it's a new, strange dictate coming down from above, or Erik making an incomprehensible discipline decision or an insulting evaluation or spot-check visit. You pick. But everybody's always angry, and it's not unusual to see people red-eyed from crying.

Terri's words about the Northton administration ("They're not really evil. They're just very, very stupid") echo through my mind these days as I watch what's being done to Better Than You. Evil or stupid? I guess it says something about my values that I just assume evil because that feels more respectful than assuming stupid.

Well, it quickly becomes clear that our supposed genius new president has no fucking idea what he's doing. Or else his pack of toadies doesn't know what they're doing and he doesn't care. We get a bunch of new mandates from on high on what seems to be a daily basis. People will be in your room every day! No they won't! Never ever have a kid in the hall unattended! No, actually that's okay, go ahead and do that! After sending down the new stupid rules, the administration seems to forget about most of them. (The ATLAS protocol, for example, never materializes.) It is the same kind of shit that I've done when I'm over my head with a really difficult class—I remember my multiple seating arrangements and ever-changing rules in my ninth-grade class way back in Newcastle. I was flailing. They are flailing.

Or are they really just trying to make everybody miserable? I think that might not be true when we have a faculty meeting sometime in late November, and Watkins stands up to address us, and even though it's not hot in the room, he's dripping sweat like he's on his fifth set at Wimbledon. He tells us that everything that's happening here is for the best, and if we're not convinced by now that he wants the best for kids, there's really nothing he can do to convince us. I feel great at the end of this meeting, because it feels like he's begging us to stay.

Then, one Monday in January, we all get a memo. It talks about how there is going to be a new definition of what it means to be a teacher at Better Than You next year. It's going to include everybody being a mentor teacher. The explanation is that—well, it's complicated and boring, but it has to do with the fact that the school has a lot of grant money attached to teacher training.

So they wish to know as soon as possible whether we wish to apply for positions at Better Than You next year.

Apply for positions.

Teachers in good standing, the memo assures us, will be given priority consideration.

Ooo! Priority consideration!

On the back, the memo has two boxes to check: one for "Yes, I will be applying for a comparable position at Better Than You next year," and another for "No, I will not be applying for a comparable position at Better Than You next year." Where, I wonder, is the box for "Bite me"?

At first I laugh at the chutzpah, but as the week goes on, I stew, talk to everybody else who's angry about this, and manage to work myself into a really unhealthy state of almost perpetual rage. It renders me vaguely insane, as we'll see momentarily.

On Thursday, I talk to my advisees about all of this. They are threatening to walk out of school to protest their lack of a full-time college counselor. I tell them how my own morale is not particularly high and why. We've had a problem this year with our senior boys, many of whom will sort of cover up their mouths, thus directing their voices to the side, and say in a loud but rather high-pitched and almost unidentifiable voice, "Shut up!" or "This is corny!" or "This sucks!" when a teacher is talking. They do this pretty much constantly in town meeting, which, as I've said, I have a certain amount of sympathy with, because, by and large, it is corny and it does suck, but they also do it, for example, in my English class, going "Shut up, Halpin!" as I'm giving the homework, and then I always do it back, going, "Shut up! You owe me five papers!" Just as with the shiz-nit thing, this is not the best way to convince them that this is an inappropriate thing to do in class. I'd like to put this down to the fact that I'm going insane because of the daily shit storm here, but it remains a big flaw of mine that I love to get a laugh from my captive audience. So there you go. Even still, I don't think I should need to apply for my job back, especially given that I have done a pretty good job here in ways that are quantifiable. (It's too boring to get into, but let's just say that due to some data collection I did on the transition program, I have graphs to prove the point.)

I tell my advisory, which contains two side-of-the-mouth shut-up offenders, that I should start doing this during my meetings. (What the hell—I'm already doing it in class.) "Shut up, Chip!" I say. "This is corny!" "Watkins sucks!" I told you I couldn't be professional in this room anymore. We all end up laughing, and the ninth-graders coming in have to kick us out because we don't notice that it's time to change classes.

Friday comes. I am doubly cranky because, in addition to having to apply for my own job—well, I mean really in addition to being denied the satisfaction of telling them to take this job and shove it—the kids are leaving for two weeks to go to internships at local businesses. So we're launching into two weeks of meetings with no kids, which is probably a special circle of hell waiting just for me when I die.

Speaking of a special circle of hell, I am supposed to talk about Dante's *Inferno* with my seniors, but two thirds of them skip class to work on this other megaproject that's due in another class today, so I end up, in a total lapse of professionalism that I've come to expect in advisory but is new in class, complaining to the eight kids who did show up about how I'm being asked to apply for my own job.

After lunch Chip asks me how I am. I tell him I'm beside myself with anger. This is probably not the most politic response. Like I said, I am really taking leave of my senses. He seems kind of terrified, mumbles something about helping me process, and runs away.

About ten minutes later our weekly Friday staff meeting begins. Chip still runs these meetings from the front of the room, but Watkins always sits off to the side, looking down, holding his PalmPilot at crotch level and tapping on it. Is he taking notes? Checking his calendar? Playing some kind of game that demands his full concentration? He's been doing this all year, and nobody's ever figured it out. I'm so mad that I am just twitching all the time, running my hands over my head, exhaling a lot, and feeling that heart-pounding, pot-of-coffee adrenaline buzz that comes from fury. I wait until Chip is done talking about how next week we're going to be working on stuff for next year, and I say, "I got a memo this week advising me that I have to apply for a job at Better Than You next year. Can you explain to me why I should work on anything for next year here as opposed to any other school I don't have a job at?"

Chip tries to answer, but I've essentially called Dr. Watkins out in public, so he puts down his PalmPilot and jumps in, obviously angry. "Every teacher is simply being asked to indicate his or her willingness to work here next year. This is standard procedure."

"Well," I say, "it's a new procedure around here, and I feel"—I'm still hip to the I statements!—"very angry and disrespected—"

He cuts me off. "We come from different worlds, Mr. Halpin, and in the world I come from, the world of regular public schools, this is the way things are done."

"I worked in regular public schools for five years before coming here, and I never saw this happen at any of them."

"It's standard procedure!" He's yelling now. "Every teacher in the building gets a notice in April!" He's referring to the kind of budget-induced pink-slipping that happened to me as a first-year teacher in Newcastle.

"That's not true. Teachers with three years in the building don't get a pink slip. And nobody has to apply."

"Well, nobody has three years experience with *me*!" It continues in this vein, with him twisting facts, arguing against things I haven't said, and generally trying to bully me into silence. It works with all my colleagues, with the exception of Michelle, who says something in my defense, and Lisa, who makes supportive sounds a couple of times. Everybody else leaves me hanging out to dry and just watches the floor show in silence, which is what people typically and inexplicably do whenever somebody says what everybody's thinking in a meeting. (I say inexplicably because I am always the jackass opening his mouth, so, for better or worse, the psychology of the other position is kind of a mystery to me.)

I get strangely calm as soon as Watkins loses his shit, which is immediately. It's like there's only a certain amount of hysterical anger to go around, and he's hogging it all, so my own sanity returns. I keep calmly throwing I statements out there; I even take pains to clarify that I'm not trying to tell him what his intentions were, only how I feel, but he's on a roll and not about to listen to me. He yells some more, bullies some more, throws some more misinformation about how other schools work in there just for good measure, and winds up with the truly Orwellian pronouncement that my feeling disrespected at being asked to apply for my own job after doing it for three years is actually disrespectful to him and that he can't believe how we unfairly accuse him of being disrespectful whenever he does something in our best interest.

My composure, which has been very loyal throughout this conversation, flits away again. I am so staggered by his chutzpah and egotism that I just have to repeat this for the record. "I have to apply for my own job that I've been doing for three years, and *you* feel disrespected?"

What really amazes me is that as I look at him, I can tell that he really believes this shit. He just has no idea why everybody hates him or why people might be offended at having to apply for their own job. This seems to weigh on the stupid side of the "evil or stupid" question, but it's not yet definitive, and this question about Watkins and company will continue to perplex me, though eventually it occurs to me that this may not be an either/or situation.

Anyway, he concludes by basically telling us all to shut up and never challenge him in a public meeting again.

After the meeting Alison apologizes for not backing me up, which I appreciate. I walk into the hall trying to take cold comfort from the fact that the one who doesn't fly off the handle wins, so I must have won here even though my school is in the hands of a dangerously stupid individual, and I've just added myself to his enemies list (though I was probably on it already—I later find out that he's got his own personal Stasi in the form of Julie, and probably others too, telling him every little word that anyone whispers. So maybe he's not so stupid after all, though if he were just good at his job, he wouldn't need the legion of squealing toadies).

Two of my advisees are standing at the end of the hall. One of them, Diana, tells me that her calculus teacher never gave her the assignment for the weekend, and can I please go get her teacher out of the meeting she's in so that Diana can get her assignment? Please? So I go get Sydney out of the meeting and give the assignment to Diana, grumbling about how I have to do her errands, et cetera, which I guess is the passive-aggressive thing I do with kids—rather than saying no, I grumpily accede to almost anything they ask for. It's my pathetic little way of pretending I'm not a pushover, but nobody's fooled.

"I love you, Mr. Halpin!" she calls after me.

"Of course you do." I try say it in a grumble, but of course I'm pleased and have a hard time maintaining my grumpy front.

"Mr. Halpin!" Chaka calls out. "Remember!" She puts her palm over her mouth and calls out in an unnatural, too high, and hard-to-identify voice, " 'Shut up! This is corny!' Just keep doing that for two weeks!"

I laugh, and they laugh, and I tell her I probably should.

But of course I don't.

I stumble to the subway, exhausted, come home, flop on the couch, and am asleep in seconds.

56

AFTER HAVING IT out with Big Daddy in the meeting, I am pretty much spent. (I have been trying all year to start a movement to call Dr. Watkins simply "the Fat Man," possibly as an homage to *Jake and the Fatman,* which is a show I never actually watched, but that's the way my mind works. Someone else comes up with "Big Daddy," and for some reason this ends up sticking.) I am very nervous about going to work on Monday. Big Daddy sees me in the hall first thing Monday morning and shakes my hand. I guess this is his way of telling me that we can still be civil. I am such a sucker that I appreciate it.

We have our two weeks of meetings. We spend a couple days on discipline, which are sort of interesting and possibly helpful, but Erik, the Dean of Yelling at Kids, does a completely typical administrator thing and turns this complicated stuff about how to best relate to kids into a three-copy carbon form that we're to fill out when sending a kid to him detailing, for example, what strategies we used to try to engage the student. So if a kid tells another kid to fuck off, that he's going to get his ass beat, I am supposed to spend approximately five minutes filling out a carbon form detailing what strategies I used to engage the student.

Our other big training comes from the Institute for Good Teaching and is led by a perfectly nice woman, but it's a rehash of material that anybody who went to ed school has learned already. And nobody is allowed to get out of it, even people who have taken this exact training before. "We paid a lot of money for this," they are told. So that's pretty much a waste of time, but at least the presenter is a former teacher and not condescending or insulting like the Buzzword Institute guys, and she bakes for us a couple of times, which puts her program head and shoulders over pretty much any other professional-development program I've ever been made to suffer through.

Once our two weeks of meetings are over, life here at Better Than You just gets worse and worse. I try to just focus on my classes, on teaching every day and getting through it, but it gets harder and harder as stupider and stupider shit happens.

We have a mediated diversity meeting, which ends up being just as stupid and pointless as the unmediated ones last year except without the screaming, and in which somebody I thought was my friend tells me, in essence, that she doesn't think white people should teach kids of color. It hurts. Hooray for diversity.

The deadline comes for us to apply for our jobs back. I do not write in "Bite me." I just check "No" and have done with it. I am really glad, because when the interviews start, morale, which I thought couldn't get much lower, dives to previously undiscovered depths. The interviews are conducted by the president's assistant for parent and community relations, Big Daddy's right-hand woman, whom I have been afraid of since day one because she is one of those people who hide their desire to eviscerate you with gooey, exaggerated niceness. Creepy. Chip, our principal, sits in on the interviews and says nothing, effectively announcing that his is a purely ceremonial position these days.

The interviews, or so I'm told, consist of Ms. Barracuda asking three questions: Do you want to work here, are you willing to do the job, and, um, I have some kind of mental block about the third one, though people have told it to me a hundred times. In any case, you'll have to trust me that it's just as inane as the rest of them. It is made clear that the teachers' evaluations do not figure in this process.

So what, exactly, is happening here? Presumably everybody is going to give the same answers to those three questions. So what are the criteria for being hired? Nobody knows. Some people leave the interviews in tears, some people say they feel like they're about to go postal, others say they felt like they were in front of the House Un-American Activities Committee.

After undergoing this systematic humiliation, candidates are told they will have a decision in three to five business days. When people get their "congratulations" letters a few days later, they laugh bitterly and wave them around the teachers' room. I'm in there as

Pam gets hers, and after Ms. Barracuda leaves, she says, "Hey! Congratulations! Lucky me!" and laughs before throwing the letter in
the garbage.

Others don't get the chance to trash the letters. Al and Glenn get
"fuck you" letters instead. (Okay, they don't really say "Fuck you."
They essentially say, "Thanks but no thanks" and probably end with
"Govern yourself accordingly," which is Smiley Barracuda's favorite
non sequitur ending to every incomprehensible communication
she issues. No explanation is given for why these guys aren't hired
back—in fact, Al explicitly asks if there is something wrong with his
job performance, and Big Daddy says no. Smiley Barracuda gives
Glenn his letter right before class starts. Classy.

This has a pretty predictable effect on people. Walking into work
every day is like walking into a funeral for somebody who's been
murdered. We're all sad to see what has happened to our school, to
our friends, and to our students, but we're also scarily full of rage.
Most of us don't take it out on the students, but it seems like the
ambient level of aggression rises. At one point we have three fights
in two days. Well, the students do. We don't actually fight—we just
want to.

I am concerned that one of my advisees is going to push someone's button the wrong way and end up on the wrong side of a confrontation with a faculty member. I close the door to the room, as
usual, and get all of their attention at once, which is a lot less
usual—most often it's just random conversation time in here—and
I tell them, "You know when one of your friends is having a bad day,
and they might tell you something that pisses you off, but you just
leave it alone and give them some space? You should assume that
every adult in this building is like that right now."

Nobody gets suspended that week, so I guess it works.

The center (or, I suppose, the centre, if you wanna be persnickety
about the Yeats allusion) cannot hold, and things start falling apart
all over. We take a bunch of new students in February, which we've

never done before but which we're doing now, I assume, because the state does a head count on February 15 and gives us nine thousand bucks for every warm body we have enrolled. Two of them disrupt their classes every day, one of them gets into several fights and then leaves school altogether, and another is a really sweet kid who can't do math because she literally doesn't know how to count.

So classes that used to work well kind of stop working when we throw these kids into them (including my beloved first period, which remains beloved but stops being the easiest class to teach and becomes a huge challenge). We don't have enough resources to provide a self-contained class for a kid who can't count or a kid with serious behavioral issues, so things just get chaotic.

We used to send kids home for saying the word "nigger." It was a rule that was held over from the five o'clock faculty-meeting guy, who, let's remember, is African-American. Erik, who has failed for three years to convince black kids to respect him because he's black and who talks about empowerment a lot (I have a very vivid memory of sitting with Diana after a suspension meeting and having her say, "I hate it when he starts talking all that black shit! He's corny!"), starts telling kids that they can't say the word because it makes white people uncomfortable and sending them right back to class. It's not long before kids are yelling it in the hall.

Martine, one of my advisees with great grades and potential, tells me one morning that three of her six college applications are basically toilet paper because our "dean/college counselor/'Mommy'" counseled her not to take the SAT IIs, and the schools require them. Oops.

Diana comes to me in tears one day because one college is telling her she has to have a letter explaining that she has an incomplete for gym on her transcript because of a medical excuse. We got the principal to write a letter explaining the situation, and he gave it to the "college counselor," who is refusing to fax it to the college. Diana is beside herself; her deadline is approaching.

I go to the college counselor's office. "Hey," I say. "I'm just faxing some stuff over to Nice Little College in the Shadow of the Famous University. Can I have a copy of the letter Chip wrote about the gym thing?"

"No," she says. "They don't need that. And in the future, refer all these requests to me."

I feel like referring her ass to my foot, but I refrain from saying anything because she's mean and I'm terrified of her. I feel bad about being a wuss and not going toe-to-toe with this woman, but I figure that butting heads with her will get me a sore head and Nice Little College still won't know why Diana didn't finish gym class.

I have a brainstorm. I go to Chip and say, "Hey, thanks for writing that letter for Diana."

"Oh, sure, no problem," he says.

"Hey, can I have a copy for my advisory files?" I ask.

"Yeah, sure, I'll print you up another one right now." I know that his brain must really be addled from his transformation into a powerless figurehead, because anybody who knows me knows that my filing system consists of piles of crap on my desk that I move wholesale into empty file drawers at irregular intervals, or maybe he goes for it because he is super organized and his desire for everybody to have advisory files overrides the evidence of his senses, but whatever the case, he gives it to me, and I run up to the teachers' room, where the fax machine is.

"Watch the door!" I stage-whisper to Alison, who's in there making copies. "I'm trying to get one of my advisees into college, and I don't want our college counselor to find out!"

Two days later the college counselor gives Diana the letter she wouldn't release when Diana was asking for it in tears. What the hell is that about?

I have an almost identical experience with our college counselor and one of my advisees' special-ed records; she told Karin that if she were a college admissions counselor, she wouldn't take a second look at her application if she included that stuff because she'd just be announcing that she was a problem student. The admissions offices at the colleges felt quite differently, and I participate in another mad scramble to get information into an admissions office without alerting our college counselor.

Every day I think it's gotten as bad as it can get, and every day it gets worse. One of my senior students is manipulated into withdrawing at the beginning of the third trimester because he's in his fifth year and he's not going to graduate. They say it's his decision, but when he breaks the news to me in the middle of my senior class, tears in his eyes, he says, "They say it's time for me to go."

One of the original five teachers of the school, who now mostly does administrative stuff, is forced out after losing some kind of power struggle that I can't even pretend to understand but that has something to do with control of all that teacher-training money. But he's team-teaching the senior math class, and Michelle, the other teacher, is practically in tears after he announces that the administration will no longer allow him to do this. "I don't know what to do," she says. "I was counting on him."

Probably the unkindest cut comes when Roberta, who has been a very vocal critic of the administration, at least behind closed doors, and who I trusted so much I put her on my e-mail list (I send occasional snide e-mails to a variety of my colleagues under the pseudonym "Lou Garou," which is a homonym for the French word for "werewolf" and the best use I've made of my high school French in years), is going to become a dean, joining the bloated administration she's hated all year. I talk to her about it, and it seems pretty clear that it's a mixture of ambition and arrogance—she wants the administrative experience so she can be better qualified to start her own school, and she believes (wrongly, I think) that she is pure and bigger than the corrupt power structure, that she will be able to keep it at bay rather than be tainted by it.

The rumor mill says the administration is reading our e-mails. It would make sense, since there are freaking eight of them and they are never around and don't really seem to do anything. Roberta is not officially part of the administration yet, but of course she is unofficially, and she is one of the few people who have the technological capability to do this, so I ask her about it in front of everybody in a department meeting. She is either shocked or feigns shock very well. I hope it's the latter—she'll need that kind of duplicity if she's going to be an effective school administrator. She says she hasn't heard any such thing and would be very surprised if it were true.

At the end of the meeting, Nina, a student teacher, comes over to me and whispers, "They are absolutely reading our e-mail. Don't you believe that bullshit for a second."

I write a fake e-mail to the *Globe*'s education reporter and leave it in my in box. When opened, it says, "Gotcha! Just wanted to see if you weasels are really reading my e-mail." Later in the day I get terrified imagining that I'll have to have a meeting where Big Daddy yells at me if they actually do read it, so I delete it. (Big Daddy is a fantastically effective bully. I remain terrified of him yelling at me, even though it's already happened once and it wasn't so bad.)

I go home and eat too much and drink too much and don't sleep enough, which is pretty much what I do when I'm under stress. It's funny—I have enough money from the book I wrote while Kirsten was in treatment that I can afford to be unemployed for a while if I have to. I know I am leaving, so there is really nothing they can do to me, and yet every morning I am filled with dread as I head into school. It's only nine more weeks, but how the hell am I going to get through it if some new shitty thing happens every day, if I have to watch my friends crying, if I spend my time talking to people I like about how miserable we all are?

When Brad came into my senior class crying after having "decided" to leave school, the rest of the kids were a mess. I gave them a nice little speech about how I know how hard it is to focus when your friends are crying, and that I was not talking out of any nether orifices when I said that because I saw friends of mine on the staff crying all the time, but that we all had to focus on getting our stuff done and getting out of here intact.

It was a good speech, especially for being completely off the cuff when I was also upset, but it was kind of bullshit. I can hold it together pretty well most of the time, but then I'm wide awake at 3 A.M. wondering how the hell I'm going to walk into this place the next morning.

One Thursday I have an absurd epiphany: perhaps God himself speaks to me, because I hear in my head a voice, not still or small but more like the kind that advertises monster truck rallies on TV, saying, "Rock." Well, actually, it sounds more like "RRRROCCKK!"

I pick up the Guns N' Roses CD *Appetite for Destruction* and listen to "Paradise City" and "Sweet Child o' Mine" (which are really the only listenable tracks on the whole thing, which is tragic, because if every song was as good as those two, that record would be like the bible of rock) over and over on my forty-five-minute walk to work, and when I get there, I have a fully formed philosophy: Less Talk, More Rock.

I announce it to my pals in the windowless basement room and cue up the two good GNR songs again. I'm afraid they're going to be appalled, but surprisingly, they are all really into the music. Michelle does a strange movement that I think is an attempted Axl Rose serpentine mike-hump, and I call out, "Michelle, did you just attempt a double Axl?" She confesses she was only trying to crack her back.

I can't really articulate my epiphany enough to make it comprehensible (and this, after all, would violate an essential part of the philosophy), but I think what it means is that I have to just teach my classes and not really hang out talking about the school anymore. I just have to keep my head down. And also bang it whenever possible. For some reason, Axl groaning out of my tinny computer speakers just sets a strangely upbeat tone. "This is going to make my whole day," Carol says, smiling.

It sounds absurd and adolescent, but what the hell, I work in a high school, and at least for a day, I talk less and rock more, and I feel a whole hell of a lot better.

This lasts about three days, and then I am back to feeling a misery so strong that no amount of rock can lift me out.

5 7

SHOULD I KEEP teaching? I think a lot about this question. I talk to some guy who runs a struggling nonprofit that does college counseling (I sent many of my advisees there to get some real college counseling, and I'm really glad I did, since they were the ones who really caught the mistake with Karin's special-ed records) about adding a writing component to his program. We have two meetings in which he is incredibly enthusiastic, and then he calls me up and tells me that it's pretty much all he can do to run the program he's already running and he's not ready to add something new.

One Sunday I see an ad for a writer for video-game manuals, and I seriously consider applying, despite the fact that writing video-game manuals is lower even than being a poet in terms of the number of people who are likely to ever read a word you write. But what the hell, I think, I'd probably get paid to play a lot of video games, and I wouldn't have to deal with this heartbreaking bullshit.

Of course, there would be different bullshit, because bullshit is everywhere, as are idiot managers and coworkers you can't stand. But at least it would be different bullshit. I don't know—am I sick of teaching, or am I just sick of working here?

Every day I pretty much reach a different conclusion. No—I'm going to take a year off. No—I'm going to start my own nonprofit to help urban high school students with their writing. The whole school is pretty much a bummer right now because the kids know that most of the staff is leaving—as people's grad-school acceptances and other job offers start to trickle in, those who reapplied for their jobs begin to tell the school to take this job and shove it, so now seventeen of nineteen teachers and two of eight administrators are leaving. This seems to activate some of the students' abandonment issues, and the fact that no rules are being enforced seems to activate their desire to break rules.

Yet I walk into my classes, and great things still happen. I continue to see really fine autobiographical work from my ninthgraders. My seniors did really cool projects on Dante's *Inferno,* and two of them are actually working hard on the big research paper I gave them. But is it worth it? Right now, for the first time ever, well, maybe for the first time since the dying weeks of Famous Athlete Youth Programs' foray into truancy prevention, the other bullshit is overriding the joy I get from working with kids. Not only because it infects the class in a variety of ways—in my behavior and their behavior and the way we talk to each other, but just because everything that used to be good about this place—the feeling of community that I praised in front of everybody at the end of last year—is now shot to hell. So what do I do?

Luckily, I get an e-mail one day that clarifies my thinking. I have two e-mail accounts—three if you count the Lou Garou one—and one of them I have had since my Northton days, when I used it then to communicate with students who wanted to e-mail me a late paper or show me a college essay over a vacation or whatever. I keep it open now just in case any former students might be trying to contact me. I also use it whenever I'm buying something online. As a result, when I check it once a week, it is full of fascinating information about consolidating my debt, enlarging my penis, working from home and making $$$, and XXX hot teens.

So one day I log on and am in the process of deleting hundreds of pieces of crap when I see a familiar name in the sender list. It is one of my favorite students from Northton.

She's just read the book I wrote about what went on in my brain while Kirsten was being diagnosed and treated for breast cancer, and she's writing to tell me how much she liked it and how proud she is that I was her teacher.

I appreciate the writing compliment because I crave praise as much as the next writer, but what really strikes me as amazing as I read her very lengthy and well-written e-mail is that the time she spent in my class mattered to her. She was in the tenth grade then and seems, to judge by this e-mail, to have become a thoughtful, articulate adult, and while I don't in any way take credit for that, I just think it's remarkable that my job allowed me to come into contact with this person's life and maybe have an impact on it. I am reminded once again that what I do is important, and I get a profound satisfaction from having been any kind of influence at all on somebody, and I think, well, yes, I hate the burnouts and moron administrators, and giving grades and having to not lose stuff, but this is a really great gig.

I'm not sick of teaching. I'm just sick of teaching at Better Than You. And I feel kind of bad for many of my colleagues. Many of them are leaving teaching, and they haven't been teaching long enough to have any former students who became cool adults to remind them of why this job is great, of why it's worth doing despite how much it can suck.

58

HAVING DECIDED TO continue teaching, I apply for teaching jobs and get a couple of interviews. One, at a small alternative school in Boston, goes really well—I get a very good vibe from the place and enjoy talking to the people. Later I find out that Zach also applied for this job, and again I am convinced that he's going to get it instead of me. This time I am right.

I have a couple of interviews at another alternative program, but my alarm bells go off when they start grilling me with tough questions about my disorganization (which I stupidly answered was my weakness to the stupid "what is your weakness" question); it reminds me uncomfortably of my initial interview at Better Than You. Other than that, the interviews go well, but everybody is really enthusiastic about the program, and I think I am just projecting waves of skepticism. I'm in "won't get fooled again" mode (only I'm hoping to God that the new boss won't be the same as the old boss), and I just cannot allow myself to get excited about how innovative or special any school or program is. I don't think I can believe in that anymore.

Of course I don't say this, I try my best to feign enthusiasm, but I think my skepticism just pours through. I don't get the job.

Right about this same time, the parents' anger over all the changes at Better Than You bubbles up into a big protest at a board meeting, and there are finally a couple of newspaper articles about how everybody is leaving Better Than You, which we've been waiting and hoping for all year. But Big Daddy, as predicted, spins this to his advantage, saying that it is really great that so many people are leaving, because now he can hire more teachers of color.

I don't think he really gives a shit about people being of color or not as long as they're willing to kiss his ample ass—he's just using race opportunistically—but still, it hurts. I know that I did a good job here and that I belonged here, but it just seems to be an article of faith among a lot of people (though, ironically, never the students themselves) that you can't really do a good job in an urban school if you're white. Well, fuck it. I'm through trying. So much for the Great Urban Educator.

I interview at a big school in a nearby town, in one of the best districts in the state. I get a good feeling, sitting around for about forty minutes with six people who seem to be kind, competent, caring teachers. Nobody grills me with "gotcha" questions—we just talk about teaching. It reminds me a lot of when I used to sit around with Jessie and talk about what we were going to do in the next unit—it feels relaxed, respectful, and good. When they ask me why I want to work there, I consider trying to come up with the enthusiasm to tell them that their district is the specialest district in the whole wide world, but I've always been a terrible liar, so I just end up telling them, "I just want to work with kids in a functional environment, and this seems like it is one." I guess I'm setting my sights kind of low—I used to want to transform education, give something back to the city. Now I just want to work with kids in a place that doesn't grind me down. Well, what the hell—I've never really tried it before.

I get the job, and people ask me if I'm excited. "No," I say. "Relieved and happy, but not excited." I guess I am still kind of numb, and it will be a while before I can work up any kind of school spirit again.

Speaking of school spirit, the tacky people who run Better Than You now are organizing all the end-of-year festivities. I kind of know that anything these people run is not going to work for me in terms of saying good-bye to my advisory, so I invite them all over to my house for dinner.

My downstairs neighbor is a Chinese chef of almost supernatural skill, so I hire her to cook a big feast for us. The kids come a little late, but eight out of eleven show up, which is a pretty good ratio. Will couldn't get off work, Cam already had plans, and Denise, who didn't speak to me two years ago, never acknowledges the invitation. So maybe she and I haven't come as far as I thought. Anyway, the kids come over, and it seems like we spend the whole night laughing. Diana and Nychelle, who didn't speak for two years, actually sit next to each other and start laughing about it.

"Remember sophomore year, and we all had to sit on separate sides of the room?"

"I couldn't even say your name for a whole year! I just called you 'her.' Oooh, I hated you!" Everybody laughs.

Karin does an extended riff on all the people that get on her nerves at her church, including a wicked parody of an overweight woman "getting the spirit." I laugh so hard I can hardly breathe.

The food is incredibly delicious if maybe a little more exotic than what the kids are used to, and they do a fantastic job of pretending to love it as much as I do, which I find really touching. I really enjoy hanging out here. I am convinced that the kids are going to eat and run, because while I do feel close to them, I'm under no illusions about the fact that I am still a teacher and they are still students, and they probably have all kinds of interesting teenagery stuff they would rather be doing. I am pleasantly surprised, then, when they hang out for two hours, three hours, four hours, laughing and reminiscing. The party finally ends when Diana's long-suffering boyfriend agrees to take four other people to the four corners of Boston and they all pile into his car. It's a beautiful night, and I feel really happy. I wish this could be our official good-bye, but there is still the school-sponsored stuff to get through.

First comes the prom. I am a senior advisor but not returning, so I'm not asked to chaperone. Roberta and Olga are asked to do the honors, since they are returning (and are therefore now pariahs with the rest of the faculty). I used to kind of consider Roberta my friend, but now that she has gone over to the other side (including giving us some really smarmy party-line orders at a department meeting), I can't stand to speak to her. I end up not being asked to the prom at all until two days beforehand, when Smiley Barracuda interrupts a class of mine (because, after all, I'm only teaching here) and says, "Can you come to the prom? We're asking most people just to stop by but this is for dinner too, the kids would want you there, if you want to bring your wife you'll have to pay, so can you come?"

"Uhhh . . . I don't know, I mean, I'll have to talk to my wife," I say, because I was just raised too well to be blatantly rude to people to their face (in print it's obviously quite another story), so I don't tell her how incredibly tacky she is and how this last-minute bullshit invitation is so obviously not a real invitation but just a way for her to say that she invited me and I refused.

"Okay, then, you think about it," she says, and literally snatches the invitation out of my hand. Alison, the other departing senior advisor, actually doesn't get her invitation until the day before the prom.

Smiley Barracuda does similar stuff with graduation. She creates this whole system where faculty are supposed to have tickets to attend, so everybody has to go to her to ask for a ticket. Now, in the past, senior advisors have been part of the ceremony, but not this time, which I find out very late and which hurts. It's part of the pattern of behavior from the cabal that runs this place now. They're not satisfied to have won—they need to keep kicking us once we're down.

Smiley tries to deny Alison, who's also a senior advisor, a ticket. Alison has worked with these kids every day for four years, and they try to keep her out of the graduation ceremony. She sends the entire management team an e-mail telling them she hopes she raises her children to be better people than they are. I'm sure she will. Most people do.

Graduation comes, and I go and stand with the class for an hour while they put their caps and gowns on. I have been to graduations before, but this is different—I taught these kids this year, and I've been with my advisory for three years. I am just glowing. I'm unspeakably proud of them. And yes, of course the ceremony is going to suck, because graduations always do, but it's important too. I'm glad to have this ritual to mark their transition out of here.

Chip has done a lot of behind-the-scenes infighting to allow the senior advisors to walk into the hall with the class, which is a classy move on his part. So we process into the hall, and in a tremendous display of irony Alison ends up sitting in a chair that says, RESERVED FOR [MS. BARRACUDA]. Hee-hee! The ceremony is boring, the hall is hot, and the graduation speaker is my state senator. Big Daddy spends about ten minutes introducing her, going on and on about all of her achievements but strangely not mentioning the five years in which she did not pay her income taxes or the six months she spent serving her constituents, of whom I am one, from a halfway house because she violated her probation after her tax-evasion conviction.

The citizenship and democracy part of this school's mission was always bullshit, but having a convicted tax cheat as the graduation speaker is really the final nail in the coffin.

She begins by saying that her speech will be shorter than her introduction, but this proves to be completely untrue, and we suffer in the heat for what seems like forever but is probably only fifteen minutes through a series of graduation banalities that are unremarkable except for the one part where she praises Big Daddy and says how great he is and how "this school will continue to thrive under his leadership, because he expects the best, and if you're not willing to work hard, you better keep on walking!" The hall is dead silent at this obvious applause line except for the frantic clapping of Julie, the English teacher; Mommy, the dean/college counselor; and, of course, Smiley Barracuda. The three women clap way too fast and way too loud and then stop kind of suddenly when it becomes clear that they are the only people in the entire auditorium who are clapping. I have worked my ass off for these kids for three years and am struck by the incredible disrespect inherent in these stupid women applauding this line from the criminal onstage. Then again, I really shouldn't expect these women to suddenly develop class just because somebody's playing "Pomp and Circumstance," so I manage to decide that it's not going to bother me tonight.

And then something strange happens. When my advisees start getting their names called and picking up their diplomas, I start to cry. Knowing what a terrible sap I am, I probably shouldn't be surprised, but I am—I expected to be happy and proud of them, so those emotions don't overwhelm me. No, what gets me is the sadness. I am just really, really sad to say good-bye to them. I know they have to go, and God knows I'm not staying either, but I miss them. Their names are called, and they are gone, I mean, you know, still in the hall, but gone really, and already I miss them so much.

I stagger out after the ceremony and hug my advisees and pose for pictures. Will gives me a really nice, sincere good-bye and thanks me several times. I don't quite know what I did, but he seems like he can't thank me enough. I appreciate it. Diana also thanks me, hugs me, and takes a picture. Chaka hands me a card with a very nice note inside. I hug Ralph and Chaka and Karin and Julia and Martine and a few kids who were not in my advisory but were in my English class, and I try not to cry, but it doesn't work.

After the ceremony, Kathleen, who as a founder of the school always attends graduation, comes up and starts talking at me. She rambles on incoherently about her sons' high school classes (her sons are both adults), and I am distracted by what is either a piece of gum in front of her bottom teeth or some kind of weird dental work. I had fantasized about telling her off, about telling her what a fraud she is for selling me this vision of a school that she wasn't even willing to fight for, but in the end I just listen politely to her blathering and move on.

A bunch of teachers go out after the ceremony, and we all tell stories about the seniors and drink to them, and as we sit at an outside table with beers in our hands and empties at our elbows, Diana heads into the restaurant with her boyfriend. Upon seeing her, we are too drunk to be embarrassed about drinking in front of students, so instead we all raise our glasses and loudly toast her. She laughs and goes into the restaurant.

What follows is just a profound anticlimax. Friday is our last day of classes, and half my kids skip class and don't get the good-bye letter I wrote them, and then everybody goes home and it's just over. Strange. I keep waiting for the trumpets, for somebody to play "Pomp and Circumstance" for me, but it keeps not happening. I go home, and although in a way I'm elated to get out of this place, I'm also depressed. In spite of the fact that the weasels who founded the school sold out the vision they probably never believed in in the first place, in spite of the fact that the bad guys won, we really did have something special. And now nobody is sending us off into the world with a piece of paper in our hands that says we did something special, and it feels weird.

I just about recover over the weekend, and then I have to go back in for final exams, which are all oral exams with members of the community there to watch and help grade the kids. We call them "juries." On Monday I have Big Daddy's wife as the designated outsider on a jury I'm running. I'm terrified, but she proves to be competent, professional, and quite obviously much smarter than her spouse, and it's uneventful.

Tuesday I come in and clean out my desk. It's a really spectacular mountain of shit, but it takes me less than an hour to clean it all up. I just throw everything away. There's nothing here that I want. (Well, that's not true—I created a lot of handouts and assignments and stuff, but I get Andres to burn me a CD that contains every file I ever created here, so I take that and throw out every scrap of paper.)

Wednesday I have more juries, and Kathleen, bizarrely, shows up as one of two designated outsiders on one of them. Once again I can't bring myself to be rude to her. I just let her take over and talk too much, which is what she always did when she worked here, and which is apparently all she wants out of this process. She takes a shot at me at the end, though. She says good-bye to the other outsider, saying, "It was a pleasure working with you." Then she turns to me and says, "Mr. Halpin . . . as always," and I know her well enough to know damn well that the omission is intentional, and I say, because I feel the same way, "Yes." It's kind of a beautiful exchange in a sick way.

And then I'm done, and once again I feel sad, I feel strange, I don't want to leave. I wander around the building for half an hour, saying to any friendly face I encounter, "Three years of my life. And now it's just over." I walk out, go home, get sad, and quickly find that not going to work on Thursday makes me feel a whole lot better.

Finally Friday comes, and I head out for the last party at Al's. I have been thinking a great deal lately about that first party at Al's where Chip cut up the strips of poem and it was weird and corny but I totally fell for it, and that really marked the beginning of this place for me, so it feels appropriate to end it here. I make little diplomas for everybody from "the Bored of Better Than You," and hand them out so that we have a little piece of paper that says we did something special. Al, as always, puts on a spectacular spread, and I eat way too much and drink way too much. There is dancing to eighties music (so we get "Take On Me" instead of "Pomp and Circumstance," but what the hell—"Take On Me" has a way better video), there is champagne, there are innumerable really vile personal sexual things said about everybody we all hate, but somehow it never gets maudlin or weepy, it never gets too bitter or sad. It's just a great celebration and the best party I've attended in years.

I feel like shit physically for an entire day afterward (I simply can't party like it's 1999 anymore), but emotionally, I feel great. At last it's over.

EPILOGUE

Nine Years and Counting

IT'S NOW AUGUST 2002. Last month I went over to my new school and signed my contract. I will be spending three fewer hours a week in class than I did at Better Than You, and I will be making 25 percent more money. And I will have the kind of respectable benefits that come from being in a union workplace. And, presumably, my race won't be an issue.

Yesterday I rode my bike over to my new school. I'm starting to look forward to working there. I'm also starting to feel that nervous terror that comes with a new job. What if the kids don't like me? What if my colleagues don't like me? What if I don't know what I'm doing?

I take all these fears as a good sign—since I've felt them every time I started a new teaching job, it seems kind of reassuring and hopeful. I was certainly damaged by the whole Better Than You experience, and I suspect that my anger and hurt will bubble up at weird times over the next year or so, but fundamentally, I'm still in the game, and I'm excited to meet a hundred new kids in a couple of weeks.

I have seen my students from Better Than You a couple of times this summer—on the subway, on the street, or whatever. It's been bittersweet; I always really enjoyed the feeling I got seeing my students around—like I really was a civil servant in the best sense of the word, that in working with these kids I was serving my city in a really important way.

I'm going to miss that. And I'm going to miss them. In fact, I already do.

But I am, finally, excited that when September comes, I'll be teaching again. I had a good talk with Al late in the year in which he said that teaching was like a long-term love affair, with all its ups and downs. It immediately rang true to me—so I'm no longer forgetting to get paid, but relationships never sustain the insanity of infatuation. So the school policies and administrators that always come with teaching have (with some notable exceptions) driven me nuts—well, lots of people have difficult in-laws. So I've just come through a rough patch—most relationships have them.

A few days after I talked to Al, I was talking to Diana, and she was having a tough time deciding between a very good local school and one of the best liberal arts colleges in the country, and one thing she told me in the discussion is that she wanted to go to the local school because they have an education program, and she wants to be a teacher.

And I didn't say this, but I was shocked to find that I *wanted* to tell her not to do it. She was one of the top students at the school, and the thought that rose up and almost came out of my mouth before I could even think about what it implied about me is that she can do so much better, that she shouldn't settle for being "just a teacher."

I have heard other people say shit like that and wanted to kill them. What gives?

I find that both things exist in me at once. I really do think this is a great job, and I can't imagine myself doing anything else. (Well, I mean, yes, I imagined myself writing video-game manuals, but I also saw that getting really old, and me getting much geekier and fatter and having to leave after a year or so.) But at the same time, when this person with what appears to be limitless potential said she wanted to teach, my impulse was to warn her not to settle.

I don't know what to make of this—clearly the endemic lack of respect for teachers has gotten inside my head. At one time I thought that if more people like Diana went into teaching, the profession would become more respectable and schools would get more functional, but now I just don't know—I no longer think I can change it, and I guess I kind of doubt she can either.

But if she does decide to teach, she won't be settling. She'll be getting a great job—hell, I still think it's the best job. Yes, it's screwed up and frustrating, but I am in love with it, and I'm going to keep doing it anyway. And in the end, I hope she does too.

Acknowledgments

Kirsten Shanks read everything almost as soon as I wrote it, told me what was good and what was horrible, and helped immeasurably in shaping this book. Also she's a total fox.

Daniel Sokatch and Andrew Sokatch read early drafts and gave me great feedback.

Lisa Graustein and Alison Kellie read later drafts and gave me great feedback.

Douglas Stewart provided invaluable encouragement from the moment this book was an idea and continues to be a great help with both creativity and logistics.

Bruce Tracy believed in me and in this book, and his insights helped make this book much clearer and better.

Special thanks to all of my friends and mentors in the teaching profession. You sustain my teaching and enrich my life.

Losing

My

Faculties

Brendan

Halpin

A Reader's Guide

Questions for Discussion

1. Brendan Halpin's first year of teaching at Newcastle High School is the 1993–94 school year. Have things changed for new teachers since then? Are they better or worse?

2. Halpin is inspired by mentors Gordon Stevens and Terri. What do these mentor figures have in common? What does Halpin take from them? What does it take to remain in teaching for twenty-five years?

3. Halpin asserts, "It's pretty easy to run an orderly class, but if you want kids to really . . . get involved, it gets messy" (p. 43). To what degree do you think this is true, and to what degree is Halpin making excuses for his difficulties in keeping order?

4. What do you think of Halpin's decision to leave Northton High School in the middle of a school year? Where is the line between a teacher's responsibility to his students and his responsibility to himself?

5. Halpin describes the tension between young teachers and old teachers. Does this tension still exist? What can be done to help teachers cooperate rather than compete?

6. Though Halpin seems disgusted with his entire experience at Famous Athlete Youth Programs, he describes some modest successes. Is this program worthwhile at all? Is having this

flawed program better than nothing? What, if anything, could have made Halpin's experience at Famous Athlete Youth Programs better?

7. How does the reality of the Better Than You charter school contrast with the school's public image? Is the collapse of Better Than You an anomaly, or are there implications in Halpin's experience for all charter schools?

8. How does Halpin's attitude toward bitter, old teachers evolve through the course of the book? Is he too harsh on them in the beginning? Is he too easy on them in the end?

9. Halpin agrees with Big Daddy's dismissal of the school's diversity training: "It would sure be nice if we all worked out our issues and everything, but how can that compare with serving the kids as a focus for our time?" (p. 195). Based on Halpin's description of Better Than You, do you think diversity training was necessary there? Is diversity training always necessary when diverse groups of people work together? Is it more important in an urban school than in a suburban school? Should students of color have teachers who look like them? Should white students?

10. At the end of the book, Halpin says, "At one time I thought that if more people like Diana went into teaching, the profession would become more respectable and schools would get more functional, but now I just don't know—I no longer think I can change it, and I guess I kind of doubt she can either" (pp. 236–37). Do you agree that Halpin does not have the power to change education? Does any individual teacher have that power? If the kind of educational dysfunction Halpin describes exists in all kinds of settings, why is teaching a job worth doing?